M[illegible] NTAE ÁT[illegible]

Great War to Great Escape

GREAT WAR
TO
GREAT ESCAPE

THE TWO WARS OF FLIGHT LIEUTENANT BERNARD 'POP' GREEN MC

LAURENCE GREEN

FH

Published in 2011 by Fighting High Ltd,
23 Hitchin Road, Stotfold, Hitchin, Herts, SG5 4HP
www.fightinghigh.com

British Library Cataloguing-in-Publication data.
A CIP record for this title is available from the British Library.

ISBN 13: 978-0956269638

Designed and typeset in Monotype Baskerville 11/14pt
by Michael Lindley www.truthstudio.co.uk

Printed and bound by Toppan Printing Co. (UK) Ltd.
Front cover design by Michael Lindley incorporating illustration by Steve Teasdale.

To Adrian Bernard Green (1919–2010)
and
740864 Sergeant E. L. Farrands RAF POW No. 136

Contents

Preface

Flight Lieutenant Bernard 'Pop' Green was my grandfather. He died when I was at university and unfortunately I didn't have the opportunity to go to his funeral.

I didn't know him very well; it would be true to say that nobody did, even the close members of his family. He was a reticent man who seldom pushed himself forward, except in support of his country in the event of war. I remember him as a background presence, hovering in a rather sinister homburg hat to press a florin into my childish hand. He was not a cold man but he wasn't a great communicator. I'm sure that he would be most surprised that a book had been written about him.

I put his reticence down to his terrible experiences during the First World War. He must have experienced a lifetime of post-traumatic stress, making nothing of it but becoming, as a result, more and more quiet and withdrawn from everyone around him.

He was a highly intelligent and sensitive man who would have made a very successful career in the Army had he taken the opportunity to stay in after the First World War.

When I was 9 years old my parents took me up to his house in Chichester for a family visit. My father later told me that my grandfather was about to talk, for the first time, about his experiences at Stalag Luft III when I wandered into the room to ask some trivial question. As a result my grandfather's train of thought was broken and the subject was never raised again.

Eventually he wrote five remarkable paragraphs about his recapture after 'The Great Escape'. He called it 'Now It Can Be Told' (this is reproduced below as Appendix 1). His whole rather modest attitude to what he did comes out clearly in these five paragraphs, along with his keen sense of the ridiculous. It is a great pity that he did not write more.

I feel that now I can give a voice to a man who was voluntarily mute on the subject of what he did in both world wars. His story is a remarkable one, because he came close to death so many times on so many different occasions, dying at last peacefully at the age of 83 in Chichester.

So, in a way, I am repaying a debt that goes back to my boyhood, and I thank Steve Darlow of Fighting High Publishing for seeking me out and enabling this book to be published.

I would also like to thank Peter Watson for his editorial suggestions, advice and encouragement. Many thanks are due to Peter Love for advice on the procedures and language of wartime aircrews. Lyle Oswald gave me some valuable observations on the Handley Page Hampden. Neil Mullard gave me some very useful advice on the rough version of the manuscript and lent me a monitor when mine suffered a fatal haemorrhage. Jason Warr sent me some copies of unpublished photographs of my grandfather in various POW camps in Germany and Poland and answered all my questions. Ian Sayer and Tim Carroll sent me a lot of useful information and photos from Stalag Luft III.

Above all I wish to thank my late father, Adrian Green, for giving me, several years ago, my grandfather's entire correspondence from the various POW camps in Germany and Poland in which he was an involuntary guest of the Third Reich. My father was also able to read through most of the rough version of the book and offered many corrections and suggestions.

Great thanks also to my Aunt Kitty, my father's younger sister and my favourite aunt. She cast her rightfully critical eye over the manuscript and corrected many solecisms. Both my father and my aunt were invaluable sources of information on my grandfather's rather enigmatic life.

This account could never have been written without the great help of Jennifer Green, my grandfather's daughter from his second marriage. Jennifer took great trouble to put many of the unpublished photographs of my grandfather, taken in several camps over a four-year period, on a disk, which she sent to me. She also answered several important questions and sent me a colour photograph of his medals.

Tom Tulloch-Marshall did valuable research on my behalf and painstakingly pieced together my grandfather's hair-raising service in the

Ox. and Bucks Light Infantry and the Machine Gun Corps (the 'Suicide Club') from 1914 to 1918. I thank him for hard work under trying circumstances.

Last, but never least, my wife, Kathi, has been a great help and comfort, with many useful observations and suggestions and constant encouragement and support.

Laurence Green
October 2010

Chronology

1887	**23 Dec.** Bernard Green born at 'Fair Home, Hawk's Hill, Bourne End, Bucks, son of Roland Green, paper manufacturer, and Jemima Green (née Collingridge).
1903–5	Served as a sapper in the 2nd Gloucestershire Royal Engineer Volunteers while at Clifton College, Bristol.
1905	**July.** Passed the Oxford and Cambridge Higher Certificate Examination at Clifton College, Bristol.
1905–7	Served as a sapper in the London Electrical Engineer Volunteers.
1907–10	Read for a tripos in Theology at Trinity College, Cambridge, graduating with third-class honours.
1909	Won the college prize for Greek.
1912–14	Served as a private in the Territorial Army in the Royal East Kent (the Duke of Connaught's Own) Yeomanry.
1914	**24 June.** Commissioned Second Lieutenant in 1/1st Buckinghamshire Battalion, the Oxfordshire and Buckinghamshire Light Infantry.
1914	Promoted to Temporary Lieutenant.
1915	**30 Mar.** Went to France with 1/1st Buckinghamshire Battalion. **5 May**. Wounded in lower groin by German rifle grenade fragment at Ploogsteert, Belgium. **10 May.** Sent back to England for recuperation. **11 July.** Sent back to 1/1st Buckinghamshire Battalion in France. Attended 145th Brigade Bombing Course

(hand grenades).
20 Oct. Promoted to Lieutenant.
30 Oct. Seconded to Battalion Machine Gun Section.

1916 **11 Jan.** Seconded to 145th Brigade Machine Gun Company, Machine Gun Corps.
24 Feb. Appointed second in command, 145th Brigade MG Company.
Attended Lewis Gun and Vickers Gun courses in Camiers (France) and Grantham (England), where he met John Dodge.
1 July. 1st day of Battle of the Somme. Promoted Captain.
11 Oct. Returned to England for leave, course and marriage.
23 Dec. Married Kathleen Dorothea Connell on his 29th birthday at parish church, Wooburn Green, Bucks.

1917 **1 Jan.** Mention in Despatches for action on the Somme.
7 Jan. Returned to France and Belgium.
Fought in 3rd Battle of Ypres (Passchendaele).

1918 Completed musketry course in France with top rating.
16 Feb. Promoted to Temporary Major.
3 June. Awarded Military Cross in King's Birthday Honours List.
15 Oct. Severe wound in left heel from either bullet or shrapnel.
19 Oct. Returned to England for recovery and awarded £120 compensation.

1919 **29 Nov.** Birth of son Adrian Bernard Green.
3 Dec. Appointed Managing Director, Thomas and Green, Soho Mill, Wooburn Green, Bucks.

1920 **15 Jan.** Returned to establishment of Ox. and Bucks LI from Machine Gun Corps secondment.
18 Nov. Relinquished commission with rank of Major.

1921 **2 June.** Birth of daughter Catherine Connell Green.

1924 **30 June.** The 'Mill Row'. Bernard Green resigns as Managing Director of Thomas and Green.
24 July. Appointed Mill Manager.

1928–39 Senior Sales Representative for Thomas and Green.

1939 **30 Dec.** Joined RAF Volunteer Reserve.

1940 Attended Air Gunnery and Gunnery Leaders' courses at

RAF Aldergrove, Northern Ireland.
9 April. Graded Pilot Officer on Probation.
May. Home on leave at Cortegar, Wharf Lane, Bourne End, Bucks.
Posted to 44 Squadron, RAF Waddington, Lincs.
20 July. Flew first mission. Reported 'missing' after plane ditched in North Sea in Tannis Bay off Kandestierdne, Denmark. Taken prisoner to Skagen.
6 Aug. First of three letters to Adrian Green from Dulag Luft, Oberusel, Germany.
30 Dec. Confirmed as Pilot Officer.

1941 **25 Feb.** First of two postcards to Adrian Green from Stalag Luft II, Littmannstadt, Poland.
2 Mar. Promoted to Flying Officer.
27 July. First of four postcards to Adrian Green from Stalag Luft I, Barth, Germany.
7 Oct. First of two letters to Adrian Green from Stalag Luft I.

1942 **2 Mar.** Promoted to Flight Lieutenant.
14 June. First of two letters to Adrian Green from East Compound Stalag Luft III, Sagan, Germany.
1 Nov. First of two letters to Adrian Green from Offlag XXIB, Schubin, Poland.
29 Nov. First of three postcards to Adrian Green from Offlag XXIB.

1943 **28 Apr.** First of six postcards to Adrian Green from North Compound Stalag Luft III, Sagan, Germany.
3 June. First of five letters to Adrian Green from North Compound Stalag Luft III.

1944 **24/5 Mar.** Takes part in the Great Escape.
30 Dec. Last letter home from Stalag Luft III.

1945 **27 Jan.** Stalag Luft III evacuated. The 'Black March' begins.
2 May. Green and fellow POWs liberated near Lübeck, Germany.

1947 **7 Jan.** Mention in Despatches for part in Great Escape.
10 July. Invitation to Buckingham Palace Garden Party.

1951 Death of Kathleen Dorothea Green.

1952 Marriage to Evelyn Haberer in Chichester.

1953 Birth of daughter, Jennifer Green.

1963 **20 June.** Attended Premier of the film *The Great Escape* at the Odeon, Leicester Square, to benefit the Royal Air Force Association and the RAF Escaping Society.

1971 **2 Nov.** Death of Bernard Green.

5 Nov. Cremation of Bernard Green at Chichester.

1. The Wild Rover No More

The winter of 1943 was long and severe all over Europe. It was as if even the weather had closed down under the oppressive reign of the Nazis. Snow blanketed thousands of square miles of occupied territory. One of the coldest places in central Europe was German Silesia,[1] the flat, sandy area of pine forests south-east of Berlin, situated not far from the Polish border.

The town of Sagan[2] was an insignificant dot on the railway from Berlin to Breslau. Just outside the town limits, surrounded by repetitious pines, lay the sprawl of Stalag Luft III, soon to be enlarged yet again to accommodate the hundreds of American prisoners who were daily captured after being shot down in heavy daylight raids over Germany's industrial cities.

Lines of huts marched to the barbed-wire horizon. They were drab, hastily built and badly insulated. Baking hot in summer and draughty in winter, they were home to hundreds of Allied airmen officers who had been monotonously informed by their captors that 'escape is impossible' and 'for you the war is over'.

Some of the grim, dirty men dressed in an assortment of worn and shabby uniforms concurred with these clichés, making the most of their rations and preferring not to upset their guards. Others, indistinguishable in appearance from their fellows, lived for the day they would outwit their captors and shake the sandy dust of the compound from their worn shoes.

Such a man was Bernard Green. He had grown a thick beard and constantly wore a beret to keep his bald head out of the icy blast of the east wind. He wore a whipcord jacket with a lieutenant's pips on the lower sleeve, a garment that had been common enough in the first two years of the First World War. It had been sent out to him by his wife in England and delivered by the Red Cross. Regimental insignia and collar dogs had been carefully removed and the Lieutenant Green of 1915 was transformed into Flight Lieutenant Green of 1943.

The jacket, although filthy and worn, was proving a lifesaver, standing in for the Polish greatcoat that Green had been promised a long time ago. Wrapped in a knitted muffler, Green would walk many times round the perimeter fence each day. He usually wore a pair of dark glasses to protect his light blue-eyes against the constant glare of the snow and, dressed in his motley items of outdoor uniform, he had the slightly bohemian air of an artist.

Walking was a way of being alone, of getting away from the fug of crowded huts. It had become an obsession as well as a form of meditation. Green was not an unfriendly man but he was a man who enjoyed his own company. He could not always think clearly in the noisy, smelly rooms surrounded by other men who often secretly shared the same obsession as he did.

Green rounded the corner of the camp, his shoes causing the compacted snow to creak. He was careful not to let his mind wander, as he had to ensure that he did not touch the low wire strung several yards in front of the barbed-wire fence. Any man touching or crossing this wire strand would become a target for the guards, muffled in their heavy greatcoats in the towers that loomed at intervals above the main fence. Green had already seen several men try to rush the wire only to be shot down with no warning. One officer had hung dead on the wire for several hours before being taken away under the cover of darkness.

To die in this way would be too easy. Green's obsession with escape involved many of his brother officers. He thought about the two tunnels being dug in various directions under the snow and the hard-packed sandy soil of the compound. When several hundred of the best technical brains of many occupied countries were forced together in idleness in an unpleasant place, the inevitable result was a number of highly sophisticated schemes of escape. A determination to get home, to win the war and to confuse the Germans led to many attempts to break out of the camp. The dogged determination of many of the Allied officer prisoners kept the guards and camp staff constantly busy. In the war of nerves, tempers occasionally snapped, and men were regularly sent off to the cold and solitary misery of the cooler.[3]

Green trudged round the perimeter of the camp. Through the stands and coils of barbed wire he could just make out the shrouded shapes of the countless pine trees that stretched away in all directions from the compound. Thick snow gave the trees a hunched appearance and the illusion that even they were braced against the all-pervading cold. Today they would offer no shelter or comfort to a man outside the wire. Better to bide one's time and continue to plan and prepare for the escape. Men were not like pine trees; they did not entirely stand alone, isolated from each other.

The biting cold kept Green walking. He had three more circuits to do before coming in from the cold. He knew that if you sat around all day you became soft and your will to endure would inevitably drain away. Men who habitually sat too close to the stove succumbed to boredom and began a long decline to death, as their will was gradually sapped. At 55 years old Green had endured more than most; he was determined not to give up at this point nor at any other stage of the war.

He thought of what he would do when he returned to the room he shared with Major John Dodge.[4] He would knock the snow from his boots at the door, come quietly in, sit on his bunk and light a Woodbine. Smoking was not to be combined with exercise. It was a treat, a reward for effort and discipline. He would take out his Russian textbook and spend an hour or so memorising verb endings.

Russian was a difficult language, but it was not so bad when you had mastered the Cyrillic alphabet. Green had become quite good at reading Russian and could converse in a limited way with a few of the Polish officers who spoke Russian. He knew that it would be only a matter of time before the Red Army streamed across Poland to liberate the camp. It could be a long time, however, and a lot of things could happen in the meantime. Rumours had reached the camp about other camps, mostly in Poland, where the Nazis killed civilians on an unprecedented scale. Despite the Geneva Convention[5] and the frequent visits of the Red Cross,[6] such barbarity could happen here in Stalag Luft III if the tide of war turned further in the Allies' favour.

Another hundred paces and the circulation was improving, some warmth combating the freezing chill that pierced Green's thin clothes. What he would give for a decent greatcoat like the one he had worn in the trenches, where the cold had been more a creeping damp than an all-out assault on the will and senses. Trudge on, swinging the arms; keep up the pace and the effort. Think of the poor devils in the guard towers stamping their feet and clicking their fingers to keep up the circulation. Better than fighting in Russia but boring to the point of madness. Surprising that so few shots have been fired at prisoners in the camp over the last few months.

Turn once again at the angle of the wire. Glance up at the goon[7] in his box but make no sign that you see him or recognise him as a human being. Like you, he has a job to do; he would happily kill you in an escape attempt, as you would kill him if he stood between you and freedom. He might be as decent a man as you, with a wife and children; he might hate the Nazis; but his job comes first. Any dereliction of duty and he is dead.

Damn these socks, they are just about worn out and won't stay up. Let's hope that more come in the next Red Cross parcel. The best were the ones sent by Dorothea, knitted in Bourne End from leftover wool from rug-making. Socks were once taken for granted; now they are a matter of the greatest importance.

Past the main gate leading into the Vorlager[8] and the cooler. The guards here have machine guns that they appear never to have cleaned. Just not good enough; a good thing they're Germans not soldiers in the Machine Gun Corps.[9] Silly of me! That was the last war, the 'war to end all wars'! Better not to dwell on that unpleasantness; consign it back to the past and concentrate on overcoming this one.

It is important to keep on top of everything, to keep all kit in good shape: shoes polished, buttons sewn on, trousers pressed. Good for morale and good to show the Germans that we have our pride. Nil illegitimi carborundum.[10] Pick up the pace and breathe deeply. Twice more round the perimeter in the chalky half-light of the declining Silesian winter day. Things could be a lot worse; we could be in constant fear of our lives, with the enemy sniping at us at every opportunity. We could be sleeping out in the open, as we often did in the trenches. We could be short of food and tobacco, not just sometimes but all the time. We could be bored and cold all the time rather than some of the time.

Never let your guard down; never become too comfortable or complacent. We will win the war eventually, nobody knows just when. In the meantime keep up the resistance, keep up the spirit and be prepared to take advantage of any opportunity to get even. Any victory, however small, is important.

Take, for instance, the phantom farter at Appel.[11] From time to time some flatulent airman would drop his guts with great force and aplomb. His fellow officers would always cover for him, always keep a straight face. Even those who later expressed annoyance at being kept outside in the snow for an extra hour would not have turned the man in. The usual suspects were teased mercilessly after the event; at the time, hundreds of stony-faced officers stood to attention while the echo of ripping leather rebounded from the wooden hut walls. Standing in freezing fog at Appel meant that the generally unfit German guards were also obliged to stay out in the cold until they got fed up and called the whole thing off, returning to their snug barrack huts and their schnapps with the feeling that somehow the prisoners had once more got the better of them.

Green turned at the angle of the wire and trudged through the creaking snow. Looking through the wire, he could see the vast area to the south that was the new camp for American officers. Perhaps he would lose some of his friends to this camp. There had been a number of American airmen officers in his present camp, members of the Eagle Squadrons[12] or American RAF officers. It was obvious that Allied air raids were increasing. On clear nights faint soundless flashes could often be seen in the sky far to the north-west from the direction of Berlin. The increasing number of airmen arriving at the camp was a reflection of the greater bombing activity.

Trudging round the camp's perimeter reminded Green of his three long years at Cambridge. He had gone from his public school, Clifton College, to Trinity College, Cambridge, in 1907 to read for a tripos in Theology.[13] When wrestling with a difficult religious concept such as predestination, he would walk endlessly round the vast cobbled space of Great Court. He always walked in the same direction; his anti-clockwise perambulations became a familiar part of the Trinity scene. When the east wind moaned in over the Fens from Siberia, he would put on his warm coat and hat and set out to cover several miles within the college confines. At the end of his walks his head would be clearer and some of his academic problems well on the way to being solved. He enjoyed writing essays and research papers, but had to be ready to do so.

In a way he was fighting a losing battle. Theology was not to be his first choice. He began to excel at languages; in 1909 he won the Trinity College prize for Greek. The means of study outpaced the end; although he passed his degree, he had not shone academically. His former plan to become a vicar in the Church of England faded somewhat as he went to work as a manager of the family paper mill at Wooburn Green in Buckinghamshire.

It would take many more thoughtful circuits of Great Court to make Green's mind up on the matter of holy orders. At least in Stalag Luft III the issue was clear: no man could be an agnostic about the threat posed to the world by Adolf Hitler and his Nazi criminals.

Green walked on beside the taut layers of wire that lay between him and a dubious freedom. He saw a small figure standing at the corner of a hut in the frigid dusk a hundred yards away and rapidly walked towards it. When he was in range, he said: 'Hello Roger, how goes it on the Rialto?'

Roger Bushell[14] replied: 'Hello Pop. All's well.'

Green was pleased to have someone sensible to talk to. He trusted Roger and liked his company.

'I had a dream last night. This is something that I would normally never mention but it struck me as rather funny. I dreamed that I was on my way home from the office on the tube when I noticed that the man sitting next to me was Adolf Hitler. He turned to me and said, in faultless English, "Pleased to meet you. You must be Bernard Green. I've heard a lot about you. . ." At this point I woke up with Dodge snoring vilely like a pig. I was amused by the dream and so I mention it to you as a distraction.'

'I wish my dreams were as relaxed as yours. I have quite a lot on my mind at the moment as you know. I can't help feeling that if I met Hitler in a dream. . . [Bushell looked furtively around to see if there were any Teutonic ears flapping] I should probably disembowel him with my bare hands on the Bakerloo Line.'

Bushell looked intently at Green. He saw a rather dumpy man of average height, clean and as neatly turned out as he could have been. Below his beret was a square face with small blue eyes and a firm jaw beneath his beard. Not an easy man to know, he thought, but a man to depend on. He liked Green's rather ridiculous sense of humour and could depend on him to keep a secret. It was hard to believe that the man in front of him had fought in most of the major battles of the First World War;[15] he just did not seem old enough.

'One more circuit of the holiday camp and then I'm back in barracks for a fag,' said Green with one of his rare smiles.

'See you around tomorrow for a spot of gardening,' replied Bushell, as he turned to walk through the snow to his hut.

Green knew that tomorrow he would put on the baggy trousers specially adapted for him to carry sand from one of the tunnels in long pockets down each leg. When the pouches had been filled, he would walk around scattering the sand in places where the snow had been trodden into mush. The skill lay in releasing just the right amount so that it would not be noticed. In some ways it was easier to scatter sand in the snow, because the Germans used sand in places to make the ground less slippery. He had to get used to walking round with his hands in his pockets pulling on the tapes to release the sand from time to time. Such humble sandmen were known as 'penguins', because of their often splay-footed shuffle round the camp.

One more turn round the perimeter in the freezing dusk. Faint yellow lights were shining from most of the huts that stretched in long rows inside the wire. The dim reflections on the snow made Green think of urine.

He could hear music coming from the one of the guards' huts near the main gate. The tune, accompanied by a badly played accordion, was familiar. When the chorus came round Green recognised the song and hummed the English version: '. . . and I'll play the wild rover no never no more'. The German guards sang quite well, Green had to admit. He couldn't make out the German words but remembered that the song was called 'The Waves of the North Sea' in Germany. There were so many cultural similarities between the Germans and the British, far more than between the British and their allies the French in the First World War. Music had the unique power to take one back in time; reluctantly Green found himself thinking about his first and last mission flying over the North Sea.

2. 'Prepare for Crash-landing'

In May 1940 Bernard Green sat in a deckchair in his back garden smoking his pipe. He had come to the end of his leave and was ready and packed to report to No. 44 Squadron[1] at RAF Waddington, just south of Lincoln.

He thought of the long train journey ahead of him. He would walk a few hundred yards with his kit to the railway station at Bourne End and catch the Marlow Donkey to Maidenhead. There he would wait on the high, draughty platform for the London train. At Paddington he would stop for a cup of tea, take the tube to King's Cross and a train for Lincoln. He did not know how long the journey would take in the blackout. He hoped that there would be no nocturnal air raid on London to delay him.

He would leave his wife, Dorothea, behind at Cortegar, their house in Bourne End that had been a wedding present from his father when they married on his 29th birthday in 1916. It was a nice house, tucked back in Wharf Lane just off Bourne End's main street, The Parade. He had heard that the first three houses in Wharf Lane had been named after Edwardian Grand National winners.

Dorothea had been a little distant of late. Green suspected that she was not in the best of health and knew that she resented his leaving for an unknown future. Despite having been married for nearly twenty-five years, they had grown somewhat apart. Dorothea was more of an extrovert than he and quite an opinionated woman. Her husband was quiet and seldom ventured an opinion unless he felt like it. The First World War had taken its toll on him and accentuated his rather reserved nature. He would have been hard put to it to explain why he had joined the RAF at more than ten years over the age limit.

As he sat in his deckchair he wondered if he would take a stroll down Wharf Lane to the river. He had always been fond of Old Father Thames. Distantly he heard a train rumble over the girders of the bridge at the throat of Bourne End station. No, he would sit still in the sun and catch the train on its way back from Marlow.

Soon it was time to go. He picked up his kitbag and rested it against the wooden fence by the gate. Then he walked into the kitchen to say goodbye to Dorothea. He gave her a peck on the cheek and told her not to worry; he would write and phone when he was able. She saw him to the gate and waved to him as he walked down to the station. She would not see him for over five years…

On the train Green thought of his son, Adrian, who was serving as a private soldier in the Ox. and Bucks Light Infantry,[2] his old regiment. Soon Adrian would go to OCTU[3] to train as an officer. Both men had worked hard in the family paper mill[4] at Wooburn Green, just up the Wye Valley from Bourne End. The war had changed all their plans and taken them away from their rather dull but comfortable home in the Thames Valley.

Green thought of his daughter, Catherine, who would soon leave the Royal College of Music in London for a safer but duller life on the land near Marlow. It was a great relief that she would be away from the possibility of air raids 30 miles away.

Green sat on the train remembering the flight training at RAF Aldergrove in Northern Ireland. On the whole he had enjoyed it, had found it interesting. Despite his age, he had done well, had come third overall, and was commissioned Pilot Officer on Probation with one narrow ring on his sleeve. More importantly, he had qualified as an Air Gunner and wore one brevet wing sprouting from the letters 'AG' above the four medal ribbons above his left chest pocket. He took pride in having shown aptitude and initiative and having done everything expected of him.

Now he was to fly sorties. The enemy would throw everything it had at him to bring him crashing to earth. He didn't relish the idea but was determined to take life one day at a time.

Once at Waddington he would learn the ins and outs of the Handley Page Hampden Mark 1.[5] He knew the intimate workings of various aerial machine guns with his eyes closed but had yet to make the acquaintance of the Hampden. He dozed as the train rattled its way towards London.

On the Lincoln train he noticed the land flattening, the level horizon now depressingly far away. No more wooded crests of the Chiltern Hills but belts of monotonous trees stretching, as far as he could tell, to the North Sea. He remembered that Lincoln was on a hill overlooking vast tracts of flat land. RAF Waddington also lay on the crest of a hill looking east towards Germany and occupied Europe.

It had been dark for hours when the train steamed into Lincoln. An aircraftman was there to drive Green the 4 miles to the aerodrome. Green never took it for granted that he would be looked after and was glad that he had been remembered. From now on he would become a valued member of a team that would be constantly changing and reforming as men were shot down and killed or taken prisoner. The future did not worry Green; he had survived so far against the odds, with a twenty-year period of relative quiet in which to recuperate. He was back in the thick of it again, once more putting his life on the line, and he felt that it was his duty to do so.

The laconic aircraftman drove Green onto the aerodrome, stopping briefly at the guardroom to show papers to the guard who stood by the barrier, a lonely figure in a greatcoat bracing himself against the east wind.

Green was taken to his quarters and introduced to his fellow officers. He was then taken to the mess, where the CO, a tall man twenty years younger than Green, was waiting for him.

'Welcome to Waddington,' said the CO. 'Tomorrow you'll begin training for ops on the Hampden. It's a good plane, a little underpowered, but up to the task. You will find out in detail what that task will be and the part that you will play in it.'

'In the meantime make yourself at home and meet your fellow officers. Many of the crews are sergeants,[6] who, of course, have their own mess. You will not be expected to mix with them socially.'

'An exhausting day,' thought Green, as he carefully checked the blackout curtain in the window of his spartan little room, knocked out his pipe and put it on the bedside table with his book and reading glasses. As he turned in for the night he remembered the time when he said prayers before going to sleep. He thought of his distant wife, his daughter, Catherine, and son, Adrian, before pulling the blankets up to his chin.

Outside, the men on guard duty checked that no chink of light showed all over the vast airfield on its hill inland from the cold grey North Sea.

Next morning Green went to lectures on the Hampden, minelaying and reconnaissance sorties and the geography of northern Germany and Denmark. Eventually he was taken out to a vast hangar, in which was parked a Handley Page Hampden Mark I. He was surprised by the angle at which it sat on the ground. The bulbous nose rose into the air many feet above the concrete, while the slim tail came down to a few feet off the ground. 'Rather like a tilted tadpole,' thought Green, as usual keeping his views to himself. Twin engines sat on wide wings, just behind which were the upper and lower gun turrets facing backwards towards the tailplane. It was quite a trim plane and far more graceful in the air than on the ground.

Training flights above the wide, flat Lincolnshire countryside were exhilarating, and occasionally exciting. The airmen went up in all weathers, by night and by day, in wind, fog and blazing sun. The high throb of the twin engines became as familiar as a heartbeat; any variation in pitch was a cause of some anxiety.

Green enjoyed aerial gunnery. He was familiar with the machine guns in the plane and took great care of them. He meticulously cleaned and oiled them, often making the rest of the crew wait until he had finished the task to his satisfaction. They seldom complained, knowing full well that the guns were their only form of defence apart from violent manoeuvring that threw the plane all over the sky.

Green regretted that he was not sharing a mess with the many sergeants with whom he trained. They were generally good chaps, who had often refused a commission because they did not have the means to pay the mess bills. Green did not use the mess very much. Being of an abstemious nature, he did not feel it was right to live it up when many families were finding it very hard to make ends meet in wartime.

Lectures on what to do when shot down over enemy territory particularly interested Green. He was convinced, in his fatalistic way, that if he were shot down he would be killed in the prang,[7] that it would be curtains for him. However, he paid great attention to the lectures, because they were interesting, even if they might never apply to him.

He learned that ops would usually take him over occupied Denmark,[8] and that his missions would be minelaying and reconnaissance. His chances of survival in a Hampden were slim if he were shot down, so he took note of the ditching drills in great detail. His retentive mind filed away the remote details so important in the event of a crash-landing.

As June wore on, Green was ready to fly operations, to fly against the Hun. He was a patient man who was determined to do his bit to win the war. He flew over gunnery ranges perfecting his aim with the aerial turret machine guns and found that he had not lost his deadly touch and was impatient to be of use once again.

He got to know his crew and to depend on them working together as a team. The fact that he was the only officer on board Handley Page Hampden L4087 did not matter at all. His pilot was usually Sergeant E. L. Farrands; observer, Sergeant Percy Nixon; and fellow air gunner, Sergeant Reg Miller. Green's turret was at the rear of the fuselage below the long tail of the aircraft, and his responsibility was to guard against flak from the ground and enemy fighters coming up under the plane to shoot it down.

Nixon was the navigator, responsible for guiding the plane over the North Sea to the target and then safely home again. Miller was the mine-layer and also occupied the top rear gun turret of the Hampden. Farrands had to coax the underpowered plane over the grey sea and occupied territory and bring it back safely to No. 44 Squadron's airfield at Waddington. They were a good team who got on well. Green was often teased about his age and called 'Pop', with the admiration of the younger men for an older man who had seen years of active service and had joined up when he had every excuse to stay comfortably at home, turning out from time to time with the Home Guard to fire watch or guard the local pub. Green noted with ironic amusement that 'Pop' could also stand for 'Pilot Officer on Probation'.

Green was held in reserve for a few weeks, while Farrands and his crew flew missions over Denmark with another rear turret gunner. By the middle of July Green's turn came, and he prepared, at last, for active service.

The plane certainly was an odd-looking aircraft, which appeared far more elegant in the air than on the ground. Its twin engines had the range to reach the far side of Denmark and come home without any diversions. The role was reconnaissance and minelaying, 'gardening' operations in the code of the day; the laying of mines was rather transparently referred to as 'planting vegetables'.

Although appearing to bristle with guns, the Handley Page Hampden was hard to defend from the air. It was a rather obscure product of the 1930s, named after a rather obscure figure in British history,[9] and was to be replaced by more modern aircraft in 1942. By that time quite a number of Hampdens had been shot down and quite a number of crews lost.

By the summer of 1940 Norway and Denmark had been invaded by the Nazis, and No. 44 Squadron's brief was to monitor enemy ship movements and to lay mines in the Baltic close to ports such as Frederikshavn.[10] The idea was to try to stop the German ships from bringing iron ore from Sweden to the industrial centres of 'the fatherland'. The Danish coast was well defended by the Luftwaffe and by coastal flak batteries. The relatively slow-moving Hampdens were a fairly easy target for keen Luftwaffe pilots before the Battle of Britain and for flak crews buoyed up by recent victories.

On the evening of 19 July Pop Green, Farrands, Nixon and Miller walked into the ops room for a final briefing.

'Please sit gentlemen. You may smoke.' The Intelligence Officer looked shrewdly at them with eyes narrowed against the smoke.

'I don't need to tell you how dangerous these operations are. The enemy are becoming switched on to our activities and much more effective in bringing down our aircraft. You know that from having already flown a number of missions. I'd like to welcome Pilot Officer Green to active service.'

'Tonight you will be laying mines in the approaches to Frederikshavn harbour. This activity is vital to limit the effectiveness of the enemy's shipping movements. You will slow him down or even, with luck, sink him.'

'Should you get into difficulties, please remember to use your parachutes. You are far more important than the aircraft. Remove your flying boots if you can before ditching in the sea. If you are captured by the enemy, remember that it is your duty to evade or escape if you can. Try not to endanger civilians at any stage. Now here are your coordinates. . .'

Green had a prickling sensation in his arms. He was not exactly afraid; this would be his first mission and he knew that recent losses had been very heavy. He realised that his chances of being shot down were very high. He would accept the consequences when the time of trial came, but would not waste his time brooding or calculating chances.

Farrands, Nixon and Miller felt much the same. They were dependable men years younger than Green but nevertheless old for their years. They would all do their best to get home to their messes the following day.

Green went back to his room. He felt fatalistic about his first mission. He would say nothing but would be ready for things to go wrong. He put on a clean shirt and his well-pressed uniform, shaved carefully with a towel around his shoulders and cleaned his flying boots. He was not a superstitious man but believed in the constant necessity of being prepared.

His affairs in order, Green left his room to walk to the hangar to put on his bulky flying suit. The crew exchanged a few brief words as they dressed and then walked out into the warm velvety dusk carrying their parachutes. Their aircraft, L4087, loomed above them on the wide apron at the end of the main runway. Other Hampdens stood in a silent line on either side of the aircraft.

Silently the crew pulled themselves up into the belly of the plane.

'After you Sir,' murmured Farrands, the pilot, as he shoved Green's parachute through the hatch. Green thought it ridiculous that the pilot should call him 'sir' but quietly replied: 'Thank you very much, Farrands.'

All four men settled into their places in the plane, Farrands and Nixon in the cockpit, Green and Miller in their respective gun turrets. Green looked down at the moonlit grass a few feet below the Perspex bubble in which he sat at the back of the fuselage under the tail boom and listened to the rest of the crew checking equipment. He heard muttered instructions, switches being thrown, cables tightening as flaps and ailerons moved this way and that.

He was wedged tightly into his turret by his bulky flying suit, with his parachute on the floor in front of him pressed against his knees. His oxygen mask hung below his chin as he carefully checked his twin machine guns, whose barrels protruded into the night sky. He swivelled the turret and elevated the guns in their mountings; they responded easily to his sure touch. He carefully folded the linked belts of ammunition into their tray at his feet and ran his hands over the guns' well-oiled breeches, feeling confident that he could defend the mass of aircraft pressing down on the concrete from enemy fighters in the air. He did not feel so sure about flak; you never knew quite where it was coming from as the plane bucked and twisted through the air.

At last the propellers spun and the engines burst into a throaty roar, which settled down to a powerful rhythmic throbbing. On either side the other planes were starting up, long flames shooting from their exhausts behind the engine cowlings. Green put on his oxygen mask and goggles and switched on his intercom. He was sweating into his flying suit but knew that in a few minutes he would feel freezing cold in the thin air high above the North Sea.

The intercom crackled and cleared as Farrands established contact with the rest of the crew. The lengthy checks were over and they waited quietly for the off. Green usually enjoyed the wait, the sense of anticipation before take-off. He appreciated the crew working as one, the feeling of comradeship between the isolated airmen, each depending on the others for their effectiveness and safety. Any nerves or sense of anticipation he may have had up to this point evaporated before the enormity of the task ahead. One could only take the mission one small stage at a time.

The plane farthest to the left lumbered slowly forwards to take its place at the end of the runway. The steady drone of its twin engines rose to a howl as it accelerated down the concrete strip to rise weightily into the night air, a dark shape turning east momentarily silhouetted against the cold rising moon. L4087 was third in a line of five tonight. Green thought ironically about the reluctance in the trenches to use a match to light three men's smokes. The first sign of flame would be noticed by the enemy sniper. The second would enable him to draw a bead and the third to fire, 'crack', and send a round through a soldier's tin hat.

Enough of such morose thoughts. With a slight jerk, L4087 began to taxi to the end of the runway, as the plane in front climbed into the night sky. There was a crackling of static on the intercom, and the aircraft rolled forwards. The drone of the engines rose in pitch as the plane shot ahead, the fuselage vibrating madly with the sudden release of power. The wheels left the runway, and Green felt the familiar pressure in his chest as the lights marking the runway wheeled beneath the plane as it began its turn to the east. The roar of the engines subsided a little as the plane levelled out, heading for the silver streak of the North Sea.

For the tenth time Green checked his guns. He was growing cold in his turret beneath the fuselage. He didn't mind; his brain worked more effectively when he was cold, and his core was protected from the extremes of temperature. His mind was a detached, floating entity that could be relied on to function reasonably well under most circumstances. Green could not explain this to anyone, but he knew that, in extreme circumstances, an objective part of him, far remote from the mass of men, would take over the running of his body, his reflexes and emotions. He took no credit for this; he did not consider himself 'brave' in any way. He just seemed to be able to do the right thing when it was required.

The flat fields of Lincolnshire fell away, as the moon glinted silver on the cold North Sea. Soon the Hampdens were flying over the water towards occupied Denmark and the well-defended harbour of Frederikshavn. In the cockpit, Farrands and Nixon checked coordinates, hunched figures in their bulky flying suits and leather helmets. As the coast of Denmark showed as a faint line on the horizon, Green and Miller searched the sky for signs of enemy aircraft. The moon rose behind their backs, and a line of clouds hung over the Danish coast. The plane roared on, part of a pattern of destruction to the Nazi war effort.

While he scanned the horizon and the sky to the east, Green thought about God. The problem was that every time he did so he came up with an enormous blank. Green and God seemed to have fallen out and parted company at some point in the mud and carnage of the First World War. It was as if God had packed his kitbag and left the country, leaving Green, formerly a candidate for holy orders, alone and confused. God might have created the universe, but he no longer played even the role of divine clockmaker, as far as Green was concerned. He held no grudge against God but seemed to have lost his address; an agnostic rather than an atheist perhaps.

A faint line of breakers marked the Danish coast. Green thought of Miller above him in the upper turret flying beneath the stars. A few scattered lights pricked the darkness that covered the flat coastal land. Soon Frederikshavn on the Baltic coast came in to sight, a cluster of lights below and in front of them.

In a few minutes the plane had passed over the narrow spit of land that formed the northern peninsula of Denmark. The planes flew on in formation to drop their mines in the busy shipping lanes outside Frederikshavn. Green looked down at the grey docks faintly illuminated by the moon. He saw acres of concrete, warships and merchant ships, tankers and ferries. It all seemed a long way below and quite detached from the freezing interior of his turret.

No enemy planes threatened them on this raid. The flak batteries that surrounded the port opened up with tracer rounds that seemed to float dreamily up towards them. Slow fireflies spread in the sky with a silent purpose that seemed deceptively harmless. The plane jerked as an explosion off the port wing deflected it from its course. It dived and rolled as Farrands took all the evasive action he could. There were more dull crumps as shells exploded too near for comfort and, all of a sudden, the smell of burning. The plane began to rise high above the chaos of guns below.

Then L4087 took a direct hit in the starboard wing. The plane bucked in empty air, fuel and then flames streaming from the damaged wing. Farrands could be heard cursing into his microphone as he fought to control the plane. Part of the crippled wing fell away, spiralling down onto the dim lights of receding Frederikshavn. Farrands brought the Hampden round onto an even keel, now heading westwards back over the spit of land.

'I can't hold her for long. I'm going to ditch in the sea in Tannis Bay.[11] Prepare for crash-landing,' he told the crew calmly through the intercom.

Green could see the fire spreading fast along the starboard wing, red greedy flames fanned by the decreasing slipstream of the plane. His turret was filling with acrid smoke, and he realised, all too slowly, that he was going to have to leave the comparative safety of the plane for the cold world of wind and water that lay below him off Kandestierdne.

'Damn,' he thought; he hadn't even fired his guns, the guns he had so lovingly cleaned and maintained for so many weeks. He knew exactly what he now had to do. He unbolted the well-oiled guns from their ring mount and dragged them back into the turret. Meanwhile, the plane was losing altitude, as the starboard engine failed. The port engine was also coughing spasmodically as it ran rough.

The flames that consumed the starboard wing were working their way into the fuselage. Green heard the other crew members coughing as smoke billowed through the narrow cabin. He heard Miller opening the bomb doors in the belly of the plane and saw twin machine guns fall away into the dark night. They were still over land and he hoped the guns would be so damaged by their fall as to be useless when they fell into enemy hands.

Once more he saw the gleaming line of surf that marked the coast, this time to the north-west. He dragged the guns up into the fuselage and pitched them out of the open doors at the bottom of the plane, from where they spiralled down into the chaos of crashing surf beneath them. Miller managed to get the doors closed, and both he and Green pulled off their heavy flying boots, leaving them lying in disorder on the cluttered vibrating floor of the doomed plane.

The plane lumbered downwards over the surf and skimmed the surface of the water. A couple of waves slapped the belly of the plane just before it ploughed heavily into the dark salt sea. A sheet of spray rose high into the air as the unbalanced craft flipped over onto its cockpit. Water crashed through the Perspex canopy, smashing Miller and Nixon against the bulkhead as the plane cartwheeled upright again. Green was flung around the inside of the fuselage and lost contact with Farrands on his way to the tail.

With an immense wallowing, the Hampden, its starboard side smashed in, settled into the sea, beginning to sink rapidly as it did so. Green grabbed someone by his flying suit and flung him out of the jagged gap in the plane's side. He threw himself out into the sea, gasping with the shock of the chill salt water as it closed around him. He swam a few strong strokes to clear the vortex of the sinking plane, then rolled on his back to try to find the rest of the crew. With a huge sucking sound the plane slid beneath the waves, leaving four bulky figures suspended in the water a few hundred yards from the long line of surf that marked the deserted beach of Tannis Bay.

Green had always been a strong swimmer. He lifted the head of the man who lolled beside him in his Mae West. He looked at the pale dead face of Nixon, whose neck must have been broken by the water smashing into the cockpit as the plane hit the sea and turned over. 'Nothing to do to help him,' thought Green, as he looked for more floating bodies. But he now found himself quite alone and struck out for the distant surf line that marked the edge of Denmark. He was chilled, and his sodden clothes hung heavily on him. As he swam, he thought of the irony of being killed by an enemy you would never see; quite the opposite of aiming a rifle or bashing in a chap's head with an entrenching tool in a midnight raid. No doubt the flak crew who had brought them down would have no idea where the plane had crashed or what they had done to cause the death of at least one member of the crew.

Green was rolled over several times by the rough surf before his socked feet touched sand at long last. He crawled through the knock and suck of the breaking waves, before rising shakily to his feet and staggering onto dry sand. It must have been about one o'clock in the morning, and he was quite alone in a strange country occupied by a ruthless enemy. His feet were particularly cold, and he shook all over with fatigue and nervous exhaustion. He had to find a fire to dry himself out and something to drink. His lips were crusted with salt, but he felt no hunger.

At the top of the beach he sat in the faint moonlight, massaging the blood back into his feet and looking at the line of phosphorescent surf curving away north and south. He had to go one step at a time, his ultimate aim being to steal a small boat and sail or row to the coast of neutral Sweden, which lay a few miles away to the north-east. The whole coast seemed pretty deserted, although it was still the middle of the night.

His body began to ache from the battering inside the plane. He knew he had a number of bruises and sprains but that nothing was broken. From behind the low dunes he smelled the acrid fumes of a peat fire. He knew from briefings that there were peat workings behind the dunes, as well as a scattering of summer cottages. Perhaps he could break into one and steal some food and some civilian clothes. He was now an evader and must retain parts of his RAF uniform and identity discs to prevent himself from being shot as a spy. If he fell into enemy hands, he would be helpless, his fate determined not by the terms of the Geneva Convention but by the state of mind of his captors. In the meanwhile he must get himself dry and rest as much as possible.

Green walked up the shelving beach to the dunes. He knew that the sun would rise in about two hours' time and that he could do nothing useful until daybreak. He found an old torn sail and dragged it into the shelter of the sand hills, where he wrapped it round himself for shelter and dozed a little. Despite the shock of the crash-landing, he felt optimistic and a little exhilarated. If he kept his head, he could get to Sweden and then back to ops.

He awoke to feel the warmth of the sun on his face. Stiffly he unwound the sail, and faint steam rose from his damp flying suit. He pulled it off and wrapped it in the sail. Looking carefully around, he sat up and stretched. Absurdly he missed his toothbrush and worked his finger round the inside of his mouth, checking that all his teeth were in place. Then he lay drying in the sun, feeling almost comfortable.

When he had satisfied himself that the beach and its vicinity were deserted, he stood up and walked through the dunes to the flat land that lay behind. It was an ancient landscape with drifts of heather, low bushes and belts of pine trees. The few small fields were deserted and obviously unworked since the recent Nazi occupation. Green walked forward towards what appeared to be a summer cottage in front of a group of pines. It was a long low house, yellow-painted with a red tiled roof and blue shutters. Assuming it was inhabited, he walked up to the front door and knocked. There must be no furtive movements to draw attention to an evader; confidence would take him a fair way if his luck held.

The house was obviously inhabited; the polished brass plate on the front door was inscribed with the name FRITZ ANDERSEN. Green heard footsteps inside and a fair-haired middle-aged man opened the door. His quick blue eyes registered Green's damp RAF tunic, and he smiled a welcome.

'Come in my friend, you must not be seen. There is no one about now, so we are safe,' he said.

Green sat down at the kitchen table.

'Thank you,' he said. 'May I have some water please? I must not stay long. Can you tell me where I may find a boat to Sweden?'

'I do not know that. I am from Copenhagen, and this is my summer home. Today I will return there. I cannot hide you here; the police visit every few days. I will take you to Copenhagen and hide you there. There are ships to Sweden.'

'I cannot go with you. It is too dangerous for us both. If I were caught, the Gestapo would shoot you. I can't allow that to happen.'

Andersen stared unhappily at Green. He knew that what Green had told him was right. After a pause he said: 'I have English shoes. You take them. May God go with you. I hate the Nazis. They do terrible things to my country. I want to help you and all English airmen.'

Green stood, and the two men shook hands warmly. Andersen opened a cupboard next to the tall tiled stove and took out a worn pair of sandals. He handed them to Green, who could just make out the name 'Clarks' inside them. He put them on. They were a little on the large side for Green's small feet, but they would do.

'Thank you for all you have done. Now I must leave you. I will not forget you.'

Silently Andersen opened the kitchen door and Green walked quickly out through the fenced garden. He walked away from the sea and the house down a straight sandy lane between spindly pines. In his pocket were some chunks of bread and a bottle of water. He chewed carefully on a crust and wiggled his toes in his sandals. So far so good; one had to take the most enormous risks just to survive.[12]

A couple of miles inland the trees were straighter and taller and the signs of human habitation more apparent. The day was warming up, and rooks were calling from the high pines. Green had travelled in Denmark before the war and almost expected to see storks nesting on wagon wheels on chimney stacks.

Looking down at the dusty surface of the road, Green saw the slim rails of a narrow-gauge line running down the side. He followed them to where they turned off the road into a yard. He recognised a peat works and decided to try to find a set of overalls to cover his uniform. He walked cautiously into the yard. There seemed to be no one around at this early hour. In front of him was a long wooden shed, where he was sure he could find work clothes. Behind a rake of four-wheeled peat wagons on the line was a hut that appeared to be an office. Through the window Green saw a man watching him warily with a telephone receiver in his hand. Green turned to walk out of the yard just as the morning shift was arriving. The men stood silently between Green and the road, some watching him, some with eyes cast down. One man smiled shyly at him, made a knife-drawing gesture across his throat and pointed to his mates. He shrugged his shoulders and stood resolutely in Green's way.

Wearily Green sat down on a large stone, pulled the bread out of his pockets and slowly ate it all. Nobody made any attempt to go near him. He drank all the water in the bottle and pushed the empty bottle behind the stone. He waited, as did the men who watched him.

After a few minutes a vehicle could be heard approaching the peat works. The group of men parted, and a blue police van drew up in front of Green. He stood up to greet three tall Danish policemen, who seemed reluctant to arrest him. One of them offered him a cigarette, which Green accepted. The senior policeman spoke excellent English. He politely asked Green to get into the back of the van, and the two other policemen sat with him on either side. They asked him no questions and seemed embarrassed by the whole affair.

The peat workers turned away and went to work. The man who had communicated with Green gave him a small wave and a sympathetic glance as he trudged over to the long shed. 'We're all in this together,' he seemed to say.

When Green and his escort arrived at the police station in Skagen,[13] Green was treated as rather a celebrity. He was given a cup of tea and some fresh crusty buns with jam. He was politely shown to a clean cell and left on his own. Meals were brought regularly to him, and he was escorted to the toilet whenever he needed to go there. He slept well and wondered how long his comfortable treatment would last.

In the morning he awoke to raucous shouts in German. Two jack-booted and helmeted soldiers of the Wehrmacht crashed down the corridor in front of the Danish gaoler, who unlocked the door for them. They pointed their rifles at Green and searched him thoroughly. When they had finished, they pushed Green back down onto his bed and shouted in his face. Green refused to be intimidated or even to look at them. He was glad when they banged off down the corridor and left him in peace. He knew that it was only a matter of time before he was taken away and interrogated. Perhaps he would find the opportunity to escape from the train on the long journey south into Germany.

3. In the Bag

At last it was time to leave Skagen. Green liked Denmark, with its oppressed, courteous people and its wide horizons. There was a quality of light that reminded him of Cornwall, where he had taken his family on holiday between the wars; something to do with the proximity of the sea that gave a clear, luminous light, popular with painters and photographers.

Green considered Germany to be a much darker place. Like the curate's egg in *Punch*, it was good in places. He was in no doubt that he would find Germans of all kinds from brutal to sympathetic and highly cultured. He had very much enjoyed his pre-war visits to Germany. He disliked the Nazis not the Germans. For some reason he was not infected with a blanket hatred of all things German.

The German soldiers who bundled him into a train in handcuffs were not the pleasantest examples of their nation. They barked at the people in the compartment to empty it for themselves and their prisoner. They gave Green very little food and absolutely no privacy. At least they let him use the swaying railway carriage toilet unmolested.

When Green managed to open the toilet window with a view to jumping out, he found a grinning guard leaning out of a nearby window pointing a Luger[1] at his head. Green withdrew hurriedly and endured more hours of endless boredom, sitting on a hard wooden seat while one guard dozed and the other stared unpleasantly at him.

The flat, neat Danish countryside gave way to the north German plain. Houses were no longer painted in such bright colours, and woods were denser. As the sun went down, wooded hills began to make their presence felt. The train roared on deeper into Hitler's Germany.

Morning came at last, grey and rainy. Towns became larger and more industrial, grimier and grimmer. Green knew they were travelling due south. The faint sunlight lay in the same corner of the compartment for most of the day. He felt stiff and sore. He badly needed a shave and a change of clothes. He had hardly slept at all and was cold.

The train came to a squealing halt at a huge station, which echoed to the shouts of porters and the panting of locomotives. There were people in uniform everywhere, from soldiers and men in black uniforms to women on the platforms in Red Cross dresses. One of them spat on the platform at Green's feet and refused him any rations.

Green and his guards left the grimy station and stood in the street waiting for a tram. When one finally arrived, Green was pushed to the back under the hostile gaze of a number of civilians. Green realised that his guards shared the same critical gaze. The tram rumbled on and on, down main streets garish with Nazi banners, round the edge of parks and finally along suburban roads lined with dismal blocks of flats.

Finally the tram ground to a halt at the end of the line. Green and his guards were the last to alight. They set off down a long road with plane trees on either side. Green knew they were marching north. After 5 or 6 miles they crossed some fields to a huge barbed-wire gate with two striped sentry boxes on each side.[2] Behind the gate was a tall brick building and several wooden huts, which had been fairly recently built. The whole camp was surrounded by a high double-wire fence with stilted towers at regular intervals above it.

The gate was swung open and Green was handed over to a Feldwebel[3] in field grey without a backward glance. He was searched and put in a narrow cell with an iron bed and a bucket for sanitation. The cell was clean with a barred window high in the wall opposite the iron-plated door. Green was tired and so lay down on the bed and made himself comfortable. He was surprised not to be made to stand up, but reckoned that his gaolers had more important matters on their minds. To them he was a sorry sight, a scruffy, middle-aged bald airman with no distinguishing features apart from the four medal ribbons above the left breast pocket of his tunic and a pair of worn sandals on his feet.

Soon the inevitable questions began. Green was taken to a narrow office, where a friendly Luftwaffe officer sat behind a desk. Green was well treated and asked many questions, but courteously. He replied with his name, rank and number but nothing more. He was surprised to learn how much the Germans already knew about him.

He was told that Farrands, the pilot, had been picked up by the Danish police, having broken into a summer villa. He was also told that the bodies of Nixon and Miller[4] had been washed up on a beach and buried in the cemetery at Skagen. He knew that he would not see Farrands again, because he was a sergeant and would be sent to a separate camp for NCOs.

Green was amused when the German officer lost his temper after hours of questioning. He shouted that Green was incapable of helping himself and that it would be a long time before the news of his captivity would reach his home. Perhaps absence would make the heart grow fonder, he thought.

Back in his cell, Green was visited by a man in Red Cross uniform. He was asked to fill in a long form and told that the more information he could supply, the sooner his family in England would know that he was alive and well. He filled in 'Pilot Officer on Probation Bernard Green 85853' and then stopped, realising that he was about to fall into a trap. He carefully put a neat line through all the spaces provided for answering further questions. He would not tell them what squadron he belonged to or what he was doing in Denmark and that was all there was to it.

The hours of interrogation continued, with different officers asking the same questions in different ways. He was frequently shouted at but never struck. Cigarettes were offered and withdrawn; the hardest people to resist were the friendly ones. But resist them he did and found some satisfaction in pretending to know nothing at all.

After a couple of days Green was taken from his narrow cell and united with his fellow prisoners. He entered a large hut that smelled of boiled cabbage and tobacco smoke. He soon saw that the hut was divided into separate messes of six men each. The room consisted of separate areas of bunks around an open space with a table in the middle. Lines of drying laundry marked the boundaries of messes.

'Green! By George how are you? Come and mess with us and tell us the latest news!' called a tall officer enthusiastically. He wore a cricket jersey and ragged RAF dress trousers.

'Dickens![5] Good to see you! How is dear old Marlow? How long have you been here?' replied Green.

'We'll take a walk in a minute,' said Dickens waving his hands in the air. 'In the meantime Marlow is fine, although they've taken down all the road signs. I wish we were there right now, looking at the weir, having a pint at the Compleat Angler or walking to the cinema down the Spider's Arse.'

Dickens took Green by the arm and they left the hut. As they walked round the inside of the high barbed-wire fence, they were free to talk without being overheard by German stooges or hidden microphones.

Green told Dickens how he had survived ditching in the North Sea and what had happened to him since. He could not tell Dickens how the war was going, because not much had happened up to the time of his capture.

Dickens told him that they would probably not be held long at this camp. They would soon all be 'purged' to other camps all over the place. He said that even at this transit camp there were men desperately trying to escape through tunnels or in disguise. The commandant was not a bad fellow and tried to follow the Geneva Convention as closely as he could. He was aware of the prisoners' duty to escape and respected it. But he would do his darnedest to prevent them from leaving the camp and was pretty much on the ball.

After several anti-clockwise tours of the perimeter, Dickens took Green to meet the Senior British Officer, 'Wings' Day,[6] a tall elegant man who constantly stroked his loudly purring kitten Ersatz. Green was later to find out that this man was unpopular with many of the prisoners because he appeared to get on too well with the Germans. But Green was not fooled; with his age and experience he could see that quite a lot of wool was being pulled over Teutonic blue eyes. 'Wings' Day had many senior German officers eating out of his hand, while he was coordinating escape attempts and winning concessions even for the prisoners who had no interest in escape. Day and a few other senior officers were kept at Dulag Luft[7] in positions of apparent privilege, to control the Allied officers who passed through the camp.

Green found out that he was a few miles to the north of Frankfurt am Main, not as far from Switzerland as many of the other camps. He determined to keep his ears open for escape schemes. In the meantime he was settling into captivity. The camp had been some sort of school before the war; the brick main block had a forbidding institutionalised feeling that was common to all countries. It would be a good place to get away from.

He was given the chance to send one postcard and decided to send it to his bank manager, telling him of his change of address. When the card arrived at Lloyd's Bank on The Parade in Bourne End, a clerk was sent hurrying to Cortegar in Wharf Lane, a couple of hundred yards away, to inform Mrs Dorothea Green that her husband was alive and well and in captivity. The news was received with a peeved relief. It was typical of Bernard to take so long sending word. Nevertheless she was glad he was safe and well.

In time Green wrote letters to his wife, son and daughter emphasising that he was fit and well and telling them as much as he was able about his situation. He could not say a great deal because of censorship; his messages were read by the Germans and by the British before they arrived at their destination. When letters did reach Wharf Lane, Dorothea would expect the inevitable officer to arrive to quiz her on the contents. There were bits of information hidden in cryptic statements and generalities; underlinings would mean one thing and different forms of address another. It was irritating talking to some of these officers, but there was a war on.

He also wrote a letter to Evelyn Haberer, a younger lady to whom he had been introduced before the war by Dorothea's sister, Mary Christina, an artist then living in Chelsea. He hoped that he would have a reply.

The day in Dulag Luft began early with a bugle call, sometimes German, sometimes British. Occasionally the reveille was accompanied by a satirical tune that showed that the bugler was undoubtedly British. On a hot summer day the playing of 'White Christmas' would bring a smile to both prisoners and guards.

Some men leapt out of their bunks with enthusiasm, their feet thudding on the plank floor as they rushed to the Abort[8] at the end of the hut. Those who lay groggily in bed had the filthy smell of the latrines to contend with as the door opened and closed. There were usually foul-mouthed grumbles from grumpy officers who had been wrenched from slumber or pleasant dreams of home.

The officer who was cook for his mess on that day had to race over to the cookhouse to get boiling water for tea. Those who arrived at the end of the queue had to be content with lukewarm water and the grumbles of their messmates. Breakfast was taken at the central table in each mess. It consisted of a slice of stale black bread with a smear of margarine. The duty cook cut the loaf carefully into slices and spread the little margarine available to him. Lots were cast for the slice judged largest and so on in descending order. Tea was drunk from tins, which were washed scrupulously after breakfast. Mealtimes could be tense and trying; sometimes it took all one's patience to keep quiet and ignore the source of irritation.

After breakfast was morning Appel. It was a point of honour to arrive at the last possible second and form fives to be counted. The guards in their grey-green uniforms stood heavily armed in front of the officers in their ragged uniforms. Behind them stood a senior Luftwaffe officer, sometimes Major Rumpel,[9] the commandant, in immaculate uniform. Men were counted, and, depending on the cooperation of the prisoners, Appel took between forty minutes and several hours. If someone was found to be missing, every officer would be subject to photo identification, a difficult procedure because some airmen had grown beards or even shaved off their moustaches. Appel was generally quite a good-natured affair, but at other times the tension in the air was almost tangible.

The rest of the morning was spent in exercise, generally 'walking the circuit' in an anti-clockwise direction. Conversations were held, plans were made and time was passed. Some men chose to read in the morning and walk in the afternoon. There was a good library in the main block, books in all languages supplied by both the Luftwaffe and the Red Cross. Green was determined to expand his knowledge of languages. He had always been a keen reader; with unlimited time he read in German, French and Spanish.

There was even a flourishing drama society, which put on plays of a very high standard, from versions of Shakespeare to the extremely bawdy *Alice and her Candle*, which was written entirely in the camp. The rules of polite censorship did not extend to the plays produced and acted by Kriegies. After a hilarious performance of *Alice and her Candle*, the actors were congratulated by a senior German officer, who had sat enthralled in the front row, on their beautiful use of Shakespeare's English. It was obvious that he had either not understood a word or was an authority on the Bard's bawdy bits.

For many officers there was the opportunity to take courses that would be recognised at home. It was possible to study advanced navigation and even gain a B.Sc. in a number of subjects. Green chose not to follow any of the courses. He had done his degree and relished the opportunity to read what he wanted whenever he could. Besides that, he wanted to escape, not to become too settled or comfortable. He did not blame those who could cope with camp life only by immersing themselves in study or dramatics, and knew that each activity provided opportunities for planning and preparing escapes.

Green had spent five of his formative years at Clifton College before going on to Trinity College, Cambridge. He knew how to survive camp life without becoming institutionalised. Like everyone else he had his black moments of near depression. This was a normal occurrence in camp life and had to be endured. The moods would pass and a morning of gloom would often turn into a pleasant afternoon.

The officers were usually well treated by their captors. Some of the junior NCOs could be unpleasant, but the officers who ran the camp were generally committed to follow the Geneva Convention and, although strict, could even reveal a sense of humour on occasions. The Senior British Officers in the camp made sure they were kept sweet, while hiding a lot from them at the same time.

The frustration of being mainly out of the war effort was always present. Most captive airmen did not feel the guilt of survival and capture to a great extent. They had not consciously laid down their arms in the presence of the enemy. Most had had hair-raising escapes from burning aircraft, some had been injured and some had even regained consciousness in captivity. Green regretted the deaths of half the Hampden's crew but felt that he could not have acted differently at any time. Had he been able to find a boat to take him to Sweden, all would have been well and good. At least he had not endangered civilians in a country occupied by a savage regime that had its hooks into every facet of life.

Late afternoon Appel always came as a tiresome interruption. It was not too unpleasant in summer, but in winter would take place in the dark with floodlights dazzling everybody in the freezing cold. Winter would become the enemy. With meagre rations, men would always be cold, at the Germans' mercy for warmth and light as well as for food. It would be harder to escape in winter and harder to get home without being caught. Meanwhile, the long hot summer days, although tedious, were bearable.

Evenings were spent outside the huts sitting around and talking or playing chess or cards. Some men even managed to sketch and paint camp scenes. The Germans appeared not to mind this activity, ignoring the honing of skills that could be harnessed to produce forged papers and accurate maps.

After supper at 9.30, the guards herded everyone back into the huts and locked the doors. Heavy wooden shutters were banged up against the windows and lights were dimmed and then switched off. Silently the Hundführer and his dogs came into the compound and sniffed around the outside of the huts, while men settled down on their wood-shaving palliasses to sleep in the stifling smelly semi-darkness of the crowded huts. Most nights someone would cry out from a vivid nightmare to be told in various tones of voice that it was all right and to settle down and sleep.

Green generally slept well, and most of his dreams were pleasant. Occasionally he dreamed that he was back in the trenches and woke up in a cold sweat. The other dreams that troubled him were moonlit nights in Cambridge, where the deeply shadowed courts were peopled by demons who howled to the moon that God was dead and that the funeral would be held at Great Saint Mary's on Friday.

Daylight hours were dominated by hunger and the search for tobacco. At first the officers had only the Luftwaffe rations, which were the equivalent of that of a non-working person. Soon, however, Red Cross parcels started to arrive with a regularity only interrupted by the Germans searching them for contraband. These parcels doubled the amount of calories and made for a much more varied diet. The best came from America and Canada and could be swapped for other parcels to provide a change of food.

Green was a pipe smoker but, at first, had to make do with German tobacco in roll-ups. He was very pleased when parcels of cigarettes arrived from home. Soon everyone had as much tobacco as they wanted, although there were inevitable delays in the parcels' arrivals. Green had left his pipe back in his room at RAF Waddington, a room that would now be occupied by some other aircrew officer, who doubtless had never heard of him.

Clothes became a preoccupation as summer turned to autumn. Green's pay arrived at regular intervals, and he was able to buy a pair of battledress trousers and a khaki shirt. He also had clothes and a pipe sent from home. His First World War tunic, which had hung on the back of the garage door for years, arrived one day, to the amusement of many of his friends. Others were impressed by the black Light Infantry buttons and faded medal ribbons over the left-hand pocket. 'There was a lot that Green had never told us,' they thought.

Letters from home began to arrive. No war news of course, but much family news. Life at home continued in much the same way, but Adrian, having failed his officers' training course, had been promoted to Lance Corporal in Green's old regiment, the Ox. and Bucks Light Infantry.

He would have another crack at a commission in the future. His younger sister, Catherine, had already left London, where she had been a student at the Royal College of Music, for a safer life in the country. She would live at home and work on a market garden near Marlow. In the meantime she had met a dashing young officer called Clive. Evelyn Haberer also replied, and the foundations were laid for a lengthy correspondence.

Life was settling down in the camp, and Green had a strong feeling that he would soon be moved to a permanent camp. Lots of new prisoners were arriving, and a purge was due. One of the new prisoners took a particularly dim view of the camp and of his treatment. To anyone who would listen he would say: 'This place really is the arsehole of the world!' He soon gave this up when Green quietly took him aside and replied: '. . .and you're just passing through, I suppose'.

Green sympathised with the recent prisoners who were 'in the bag', but every man had to accept his situation and adapt in any way he could. It was harder on some than others. A few saw it as a positive relief from constant danger. They had done their bit and would see the war out in relative comfort. It would have been easy for Green to have taken this line, but he was determined to keep up the struggle and to get out of the damn place. In his experience, actions always shouted louder than words. The day of transfer finally arrived. Green had got to know quite a number of fellow prisoners and had become very interested in amateur dramatics. Apart from his appreciation of good plays, well produced and acted, he could see the potential for developing escape plans: costumes, papers, and so on.

With some reluctance Green left Dulag Luft under the usual two-man guard. On a dull autumn day he was marched out of the gate and down the long straight road to the tram stop. He had left the camp a few times before on parole walks. While not breaking the terms of his parole, he had done a reconnaissance of the surrounding countryside and reported back with the information to the senior officers in the camp. Now here he was kicking through the wet leaves, a little thinner than when he had arrived, but fit and determined to take any reasonable opportunity to escape. He would not jump from a fast-moving train; a friend had tried that recently and had been killed outright by the fall. He would bide his time and curb his impatience.

The guards were bored and not looking forward to the long train journey ahead of them. They would not tell Green where they were taking him; that was obviously against orders. They were not unfriendly and treated their charge quite well, even buying him a watery beer at the station buffet. Green thought that they could quite easily have been British Tommies had they not worn German uniform. Neither wore the SA chevron on his sleeve.[10] Green could recognise a conscript when he saw one.

They stood on the crowded platform in the echoing station with its dingy overall roof. The train was not yet in, and Green watched while a train of closed vans rumbled slowly through the station. On one of the vans someone had chalked a six-pointed star. A limp hand hung lifelessly out of a hole in the side of the van. Green understood what was going on and felt suddenly angry. His two guards seemed embarrassed by this slow train full of secrets that no one could be bothered to hide any longer. They shrugged their shoulders and offered Green a cigarette, as if to say that it had nothing to do with them.

At last their train arrived. It had no indication of its destination, and Green and his guards climbed aboard, pushing Green's kit ahead of them. With a shrill whistle and clouds of black smoke, the heavy train left the station and ran through the dreary suburbs in a northerly direction. Green looked out of the dirty window at flat countryside dragging past as the train turned finally to the east. He felt desolate; the long rays cast by the sinking sun did nothing to improve his mood.

The night crept by with fitful sleep and lengthy waits in sidings. After one more day and night Green and his guards climbed down onto a weedy platform. Looking around, Green reckoned that they were somewhere in northern Poland. He had travelled a lot before the war, finding sources of wood pulp for the mill, and had always taken a great interest in his surroundings.

After a few crusts and some ersatz coffee at the station, the three men marched across interminable flat fields to the inevitable barbed-wire gate with striped sentry box beside it. Green learned that the camp was called Stalag Luft II and was at Litzmannstadt in Poland. Inside were the usual rows of drab huts. These were newly built and smelled of sawn pine and resin. This was to be his home for the winter of 1940 and the spring of 1941. He was welcomed into a mess and met a few old friends, in particular a man named Carr, who produced plays of a very high standard.

It was a lovely autumn. Green had to content himself with the constantly changing cloudscape and fiery sunsets. He reckoned that, being away from the Gulf Stream, the climate was more extreme. For the moment he enjoyed warm days and cold nights. Soon that would all change. He wondered if he would see the Northern Lights.

Life dragged on not altogether unpleasantly. Green became famous for his bread puddings, which he made for his mess as often as he could. Red Cross parcels arrived with a regularity that emphasised the institutionalisation of the whole German prisoner-of-war system. In a way they were a long way from the war. In reality, preparations for further German offensives were planned. Green could see that some of the new guards had already been wounded and were very happy with their dull postings in Poland.

There were not many escape attempts. Those that happened tended to be spur-of-the-moment actions, opportunistic and desperate. The recaptured men spent two or three weeks in the cooler, where they shivered in complete boredom on a meagre diet. For some it was a welcome release from communal life. Cigarettes were smuggled in and hidden in hollowed-out table and chair legs, fooling the Germans and boosting morale. One cooler inmate even offered his guard a smoke as he was escorted out of the cooler back into the compound. It was accepted in good humour.

Rumours were growing that a new camp was being built somewhere back in Germany.[11] It would be for Allied Air Force officers and would be enormous. The fact that so many were now being captured meant that the bombing campaign was intensifying. If only the Americans would enter the war at this point, what a difference it would make.

There were American officers in the camp from the Eagle Squadron and various other RAF squadrons. They were a great addition to camp life and got on well with everybody. There were many Polish officers. Green found out from one of them exactly where he was. In the camp library he found a book with maps that had been overlooked by the censor. He carefully cut out the maps and hid them in a secret place in the wall of his hut. From the map of Poland he saw how difficult it would be to escape and get home in the depths of winter.

Life at home continued. The Battle of Britain was over and the blitz on London and other major cities had begun. Bourne End, 30 miles west of London, was at risk, but so far nothing had happened to disrupt the relatively tranquil life beside the Thames. Adrian had been posted to Northern Ireland and Catherine was working at Westhorpe Market Garden near Marlow. Everyone had to get around on bicycles, and spare parts were getting hard to find. A war on rabbits had begun; they were not rationed and were a very useful addition to a working diet.

Green could not believe how cold the Polish winter became. The huts, although draughty, were reasonably warm. Evil-smelling lignite, brown coal, was used for heat and cooking. Sometimes it was in short supply, and men sat huddled in blankets in their cold huts in the evening.

During the day there was skating. A low-lying area was dug out and flooded in an arrangement worked out between the Senior British Officer and the Germans. A few tools vanished in the ensuing chaos, but a good time was had by all. A few broken bones resulted from clumsy skating; the increased activity did everybody good. Green had his daily skate or 'slide', as he called it. It reminded him of cold winters in Cambridge.

Spring finally came round. The pretty clouds were back in the sky, but the compound was foul with slush. Vegetable gardens were dug and a few crops planted with the commandant's blessing. He liked to see his charges well occupied. He was a humane man and quite liked most of the officers in his camp. British people were far superior to Slavs and other subjugated people in his opinion. He was unaware of the source of much of the soil in the plots. Tunnels were started, and the excavated soil was spread by 'penguins', men with baggy trousers who shuffled around releasing earth from specially made bags hidden up their trouser legs. Green volunteered for this duty. It needed a steady nerve and constantly filthy socks. The amount of 'dhobying'[12] increased a lot in the early months of 1941.

In the spring of 1941 Green and a group of prisoners were purged to Stalag Luft 1.[13] A long train journey took them due west into northern Germany, where they were marched to Barth and onto a sandy spit that projected into the Baltic. It was the usual type of compound: miles of wire, goon boxes, dusty huts and a constant wind from the sea, which lay just out of sight. Once again the camp clustered round a large central building, which had once been a school, reformatory or agricultural college.

Green was lucky to have been moved with a number of his friends. Dickens from Marlow and Carr, the theatre man, had been purged too, and Green was glad of their company. Life returned to relative normality, with walks around the perimeter, letters from home and Red Cross parcels. The library was quite good; Green read Don Quixote in Spanish. He found it quite a challenge but felt that it kept his mind alive. Soon he realised that he had been a prisoner for a whole year. He worked hard on his fitness, determined to escape as soon as the opportunity presented itself.

The hot Baltic summer with its magnificent cloud formations slowly gave way to another cold northern winter. Ice skating and plays were all the rage. Green studied German and Russian and was eventually purged once again the following year to the new Stalag Luft III at Sagan.

He found the camp spacious but the view limited to walls of pine trees on all sides. He was in the East Compound and could hear the sound of trains a few hundred yards behind the dense screen of trees. He could also see the sloping roof of a huge building, which appeared to be some sort of grain silo near the station. The possibilities of escape from this new camp were probably better than from anywhere so far. He estimated that he was somewhere south-east of Berlin and that it could not be more than a hundred miles to the Czech border. He had found another book in the library that still contained maps of Europe. Once again the censors had not done their tedious job properly, and Green carefully cut the maps out and hid them in a secret place under the hut floor.

He was delighted to see someone he recognised one day while walking beside the wire.

'Hey, Pop, how are you doing?' said a tall man, as he walked rapidly over to clasp Green's hand. His American accent was incongruous for someone in worn battledress with a major's crown on his shoulder.

'Hello Johnnie. I heard that you were at Dulag but never came across you. What on earth are you doing here?'

'It's a long story Bernard. I was captured after Dunkirk, escaped in Holland and was handed over to the Luftwaffe. I've been changing horses all my life so here I am. Let's take a walk round this delightful camp.'

Major Dodge was from New York City. He was tall and upright with a dark moustache and receding hairline. He shared Green's sense of humour, had a booming laugh and a good singing voice. Why he was in a camp for airmen was a mystery to almost everyone but himself.

'Escape is always on my mind,' said Green. 'I expect it's the same with you.'

'Dead right, Bernard. A few of us, Day, Bushell, and a number of others got out through a tunnel from Dulag. We were all recaptured but it tied up a lot of Germans for quite a long time. We're all here together and I'm still helping "Wings" Day with the running of the camp and, of course, with escape plans. I'm determined that my next escape attempt will get me home. I've been in the bag for over two years now and I'm getting kind of restless.'

'Same as me, John. I haven't had much chance to do much about escaping. You may be the man I'm looking for. If you can use me for anything in the escape line, then please count me in. I'm quite a good penguin. I had a little experience of that at Barth. I'm delighted to see you again. Remember the machine-gun course we did at Grantham in early 1916?'

'I most certainly do. I'd just come home from Gallipoli and transferred to the Army. I'd become a British citizen and recovered nicely from the wound that Johnny Turk had given me. Who'd have thought that we'd be wallowing in the Somme a few short months later. . .'

That night, as Green lay in his bunk listening to the snores and whistles of sleeping men, he cast his mind back to the First World War. It was the first time he had thought of it for a very long time, and he felt the burden of the memories acutely.

4. In the Trenches

Ploegsteert Wood, May 1915, and spring in Belgium at last. The mud was not quite so chilled, and the few trees that remained in 'Plugstreet Wood' were in partial leaf. A few birds sang shrilly, and the stalemate continued.

Lieutenant Green of the Ox. and Bucks Light Infantry was used to living underground. He shared a stuffy bunker with several other officers, with whom he got on reasonably well. There was not a great deal to do: inspect the men, post sentries, detail men to dig saps out towards the enemy lines, make sure the rations came at regular intervals, write the inevitable letters to grieving parents and wives telling the same old lies: 'Your husband/son died instantly, he did not suffer.' 'He died leading his men, a true hero.' 'He was totally selfless, putting his comrades' safety before his own.'

Sometimes he had the chance to lead a reconnaissance or even a fighting patrol into no-man's-land after dark, often bringing back some terrified German prisoner who was convinced that he was about to be shot. This did quite a lot to relieve the tension that would build up, with enemy shelling and snipers felling unsuspecting soldiers whose attention had wandered for a second from the dirty tedium of the trench.

One dull May morning Green inspected the men standing down before the new watch took their positions on the fire step. It had been a quiet night except for a German raid, which had been repulsed with only two men lightly wounded. If the screaming agony of a torn arm could be described as 'lightly wounded', then Green wondered what constituted a serious wound. One day he was to find out.

Green spent the morning in the dugout drinking gritty tea and writing reports. He rested in the afternoon, because he was due to go out on a recce patrol at midnight.

At four in the afternoon he emerged into the trench to plan the raid with Captains Reynolds and Bowyer and to explain to the section of men what they were to do. The two groups, officers and other ranks, stood a few feet apart in the trench. The three officers hunched over a torn trench map, while the men sat quietly with their sergeant awaiting orders.

The crackle of small-arms fire from the direction of the German trenches alerted the soldiers that an attack was imminent. Before anyone had the chance to move, two rifle grenades flew into the trench and exploded in a sheet of white flame. There was a second's silence in which the rifle shots seemed to recede.

Green lay on the duckboard on his right arm. Someone was sitting on his head. He heard a groan and felt a fiery pain just above his right hip. He realised that the groan had come from him, as he heard gasps and shrieks from other men.

Captain Bowyer shifted his weight from Green's head and muttered 'Mother', as he clutched his shattered hand to his chest. Captain Reynolds was unconscious; blood was seeping from his open mouth. Green called in a shaky voice for stretcher-bearers, as hot brass cartridge cases cascaded all over him from riflemen firing on either side. The concussion of their shots made his head throb unbearably. He noticed that the Lewis gun was firing short bursts and that the enemy fire seemed to be slackening off. Perhaps Jerry was on his way back to his own trenches.

Eventually the officers and men were stretchered away by grim bearers and laid down at the forward dressing station in the wood. Green experienced intense pain as his torn leather jerkin was removed and his clothes cut away from his wound. He had lost quite a lot of blood and felt weak and slightly delirious. 'What would the platoon do without me?' he wondered. He was told that his wound was painful but not serious, a 'light' wound. He would be sent to the rear and given time to heal, probably at home.[1] 'That was that,' he thought as he sank into a deep sleep.

After the war he would wear the torn leather jerkin with its blood patches to work in the garden at Cortegar. He knew that the sight of the rough garment worried and upset Dorothea, but he could not explain to her, or to himself, why he insisted on wearing it.

Green noticed the scrabble of bony feet in the walls of the hut in Stalag Luft III. He remembered the rats that were also everywhere in the trenches. They were considered to be in league with the enemy and were usually referred to by Green and his fellow officers as 'Ratsen'.

They had not been much of a problem at the beginning of the war, tending to keep their distance. After the slaughter on the Marne, they increased and became bolder. They began to gorge on the flesh of the dead and greedily invaded the trenches. The first indication of their menace was Corporal Emmett waking up to find a rat chewing his nose. He had to be sent back for treatment, and the ribbing he endured from his comrades made him a sour and grumpy soldier.

Green would always remember probing the remains of a wood near the River Ancre, which had been the scene of heavy and repeated fighting over a long period. Human remains lay around: helmets, limbs, water bottles and bones. It was a still landscape until one walked through it. Then with a vicious rustle hundreds of fat rats ran away from arms, heads and pelvises that lay at random on the churned ground. Here half a German soldier, green in colour, lay propped against a tree; there a pair of khaki legs sprawled on their own, puttees and boots immaculate. The rats had done but half a job of clearance; but Green scarcely noticed the smell of death any more.

Back in the trench, Green was used to the patter of tiny feet over his blanket at night. He kept his hands and face covered, however, just in case the supply of fresh corpses was to dry up in no-man's-land.

One day the rats robbed Green and his men of a friend. Part of the parados[2] of the trench consisted of long-dead soldiers. Green was reconciled to their presence and reckoned that they were there because they still had a job to do. From the helmets that were gradually emerging from the side of the trench, he estimated that about half the corpses were British and half German. There was even a skull in a French helmet that rolled out of the side of the trench one morning at breakfast.

Before setting out on a patrol, Green and his men would solemnly shake a hand that stuck out of the earth. It was quite intact and contained in a black leather glove. The gesture was not meant as a blasphemous action but rather as a salute, a familiarisation with death that was all around them and could claim any of them at any time. One evening the rats ate the leather of the glove and all that remained of the hand was a small pile of finger bones and some strips of leathery skin on the duckboard. Green felt that he had lost an old friend. Something constant and dependable had gone, reminding Green that, even though trench life was monotonous to the point of madness, it could all change for the worse in a matter of seconds.

Back home in Bourne End, Green had done something to get his own back on the rats. He had trapped one and then carefully stuffed and mounted it in a lifelike pose. It was his first foray into taxidermy and had fascinated Adrian, his young son, and horrified Dorothea, who told him in no uncertain terms that being in the Army had coarsened him.

The smells and sounds of the war had never left Green. He had been in action when the Germans had first used chlorine gas. He could see it drifting in a yellowish-green cloud towards his position, hugging the ground and swirling round shell holes. He had swung his trench rattle and shouted 'gas, gas, gas' before putting on his clumsy respirator and supervising his gun team with theirs.

Other soldiers had not been as lucky or as well prepared. Clumps of them writhed on the ground foaming at the mouth, their sightless eyes rolling in their heads. Some of these men would survive; most would die soon, or years later from complications. Green did not want to remember many of these scenes, but they continued to visit him in dreams as clearly as if he were still on the Somme or at Ypres.

There were pleasanter memories, but Green wondered how illusory they were. He remembered his honeymoon at Christmas in 1916. He had married Dorothea on his 29th birthday, two days before Christmas. His father, Roland, owner of the paper mill at Wooburn Green and churchwarden there for many years, had given him the detached house Cortegar in Wharf Lane, the pretty road leading down to the river. Green had been delighted at his generosity and had moved straight in with his new bride. If only his life had continued in this fortunate vein.

A few days into the new year and quite soon before Green was to return to France, a letter came from the War Office. Green had been awarded a Mention in Despatches, a recognition of his bravery and initiative during the Battle of the Somme the previous year. He felt pleased that he had been recognised as an effective officer. It did something to allay his doubts about the part he was playing in the 'war to end all wars'.

He had been promoted to Captain on 1 July 1916, the first day of the Battle of the Somme, the 'big push' that was supposed to make the stalemate of the previous eighteen months a thing of the past. His company had been in reserve just outside Hébuterne, at the northern end of the battlefield. At the end of the day the Colonel had sent for Green.

'The day has not gone well for us Green,' said the Colonel.'We have made forward progress in some sectors, none in others. The stalemate is not yet broken; there is much hard fighting to be done. Our losses far exceed expectations. Today could be the worst day in the history of the British Army from the point of view of casualties.[3]

'It is obvious that the bombardment has neither wiped out the

German trenches nor cut the enemy wire sufficiently to enable us to advance to our goals. We shall win, but it will take longer than we had previously thought.'

'The losses in the Machine Gun Corps have been particularly heavy. You have acted well in the past and I am promoting you to Captain with immediate effect. Draw the extra pips from the QM sergeant and have your batman sew them on as soon as possible. And good luck.'

Green rose to his feet, put on his cap, and saluted smartly. The salute was returned and Green said: 'Thank you Sir.' He then turned and climbed the steps that led out of the bunker into the violet-tinted evening.

The Colonel turned to his adjutant and said: 'A man of few words but a good one. To win this war we need more like him.'

Green's hearing was fairly acute. He did not know what to think or feel at the end of this long and boring day. The days to come would turn out to be very different. Before turning in, he checked his gun teams and supervised the cleaning of the Vickers guns.

As he sat with a mug of tea in the trench, he thought of the irony of now being in charge of a Vickers gun company. With his keen sense of the ridiculous, he noted the fact that he, once apparently destined to become a vicar, now commanded a number of Vickers machine guns, whose role was to kill as many German-speaking men as possible. He had somehow become the vicar of death in a far from vicarious role.

He had been fighting in France and Belgium for almost a year and a half. His greatest preoccupation was not showing fear and leading from the front. He felt intense fear before an attack; even though he did not consider himself a particularly imaginative man, he found himself sweating and dry mouthed. So he told himself that he was smoking too much and drinking too much stewed tea. The truth of the matter is that he did not want to let his men down by being 'windy'. His senior NCOs knew when to leave him alone and when to brace him up by his quiet and unusually withdrawn demeanour.

When the action began, his fear slipped off like a gas cape. He became inwardly calm, and his mind worked with icy deliberation. Caring deeply about his men, he tried to make sure that they were subjected to no unnecessary risks.

Most of the soldiers under him were country men: chair bodgers,[4] foresters, farm workers, gamekeepers and poachers. Most spoke with the accents of their home counties, usually Buckinghamshire or Oxfordshire. There were a number of rogues in his command, scroungers and liars, but most performed well in a tight spot. Green felt bad when men were killed, and worse when they were men whom he had disliked. He tried to have no favourites and to treat everyone the same. His nickname in the trenches was 'Fat Aunty', a soubriquet of which he was rather proud, because it revealed his caring attitude to the men under his command.

He knew that he had a temper but made sure that he rarely lost it, often hiding his displeasure under a taciturn façade. When he let go, it was always to good effect, certainly not a case of 'sound and fury signifying nothing'. Habitually bad-tempered officers were universally known as 'the Barber's Cat', because they were 'full of wind and piss'.

He had ceased to worry too much about his own safety. His worries were minor; his loss of hair was a problem, as was the fact that he had Dorothea to think about. It would not be fair to her if he were to be blown into a thousand pieces or drown in the depths of a mud hole. As usual he did not want to let anyone down or be a cause of their misery.

It was hard for him to remember a world where one took the train to work every day and came home to be looked after in the evening, when going for a country walk did not involve working out cover and arcs of fire. It was difficult to imagine being clean and wearing clean linen and clothes that did not smell, drinking tea that did not taste of petrol and going down to the pub for a pint of good English beer.

Above all, there was the fighting back and forth over an increasingly churned and featureless landscape, instructing a gun team to set up in the shell hole just beyond the dead German officer with no head.

One typical day that Green remembered started with cold pre-dawn drizzle. During the usual morning briefing in the trench Green had turned to his company sergeant major to tell him to keep awake. Seeing that he had his head down, Green put his hand on his shoulder to wake him up with a mild reproach. But there was no life in the eyes that stared at Green in surprise. A neat hole had been drilled through the side of the man's tin hat; Green had not even heard the shot that had just killed him. A freak gap in the sandbags had allowed the sniper's round to find its mark as if by chance.

The rest of the day went no better. Green directed his gun teams to support the attack on the splintered remains of what had once been a wood. Losses were high and when they reached the wood it was to find that the German front trench had been abandoned with a number of booby traps set under dead soldiers. Fortunately no one was fooled, but the German counter-attack through the thick drizzle caught almost everyone by surprise.

Slipping and sliding, cursing and swearing, the gun teams staggered back to their own trench under covering fire from the riflemen. A number were shot down by enemy small-arms fire before the German artillery started to rain down shells on them with uncanny accuracy. Green's throat was raw with shouting orders and directions and with the burning taste of cordite. Just before reaching the cover of his own trench, Green sprawled full length in the sticky mud. As he went down he felt something rip across the front of his tunic.

Back in the trench, Green was requested to report to the Major.

'Not a good day Green,' were the Major's terse words. 'Just remember that the machine guns are supposed to support the troops, not the other way round.'

Green could see the strain and fatigue in the older man's face and smell the whisky on his breath. He supposed that he had to vent his frustrations on somebody.

'Before you go, get yourself smartened up! Get that strap repaired and your tunic sewn up. It just won't do you know. . .'

Green looked down at his muddy tunic, at the frayed furrow ploughed across the serge and the severed brown leather strap hanging below his Sam Browne on the right-hand side.[5]

'Certainly sir, I'll make sure it doesn't happen again,' he replied. The frosty look on the Major's face showed that the irony contained in Green's reply had not been wasted.

In June 1918 Green had been awarded the Military Cross in the King's birthday honours. The news came as a surprise; his first cousin, Ralph Barcham Green, an officer in the Royal West Kents, had won his MC, but Green had never considered that he was up for one. He wore the diminutive white and violet ribbon with pride but was at a loss to say what specifically it had been awarded for. When asked, he would say: 'It came with the rations.' That would end the speculation, but Green was glad that he had it; it proved that he must have done something right in the trenches.

5. Escape Plans

'A penny for your thoughts, Bernard.' The quiet American voice raised Green from his distant reverie and brought him back to the present as he sat on the warm step of the hut in the dying glow of an summer evening. He was back in the camp in a flash, relieved to be somewhere safe and familiar. He squinted his eyes against the falling sun.

'At least there are trees around here. The trouble is that they are as far away from us as the Somme,' said Green.

'There's someone I'd like you to meet. We'll walk over to his hut now if that's OK,' replied Dodge. Once inside the hut, Dodge and Green took off their caps and knocked quietly on one of the doors.

'Come in,' called a voice with a faint South African accent. A dark, intense man opened the door. He had a mop of untidy hair, a piercing gaze and a scar running from the corner of one eye.

'This is Roger, otherwise known as Squadron Leader Bushell. Big X to a few of us. He is in charge of all escapes from this camp. Obviously all this information is to be kept under your hat. We can use you in some capacity in forthcoming escape plans.'

'I would be delighted to help in any way I can. I've previously done some penguin work and I'm very good at keeping my trap shut,' replied Green, pleased to be involved once again.

Bushell looked shrewdly at Green. He saw a four-square man of average height with faded blue eyes and a determination that had been in no way diminished by three long years in the bag. His next question took Green by surprise.

'I hear that being here in the camp takes you away from an unhappy home life.'

Green replied in an unhurried manner, recognising an old barrister's trick designed to knock the subject off his guard.

'I wouldn't exactly say that. And I don't rattle easily. In any case, I don't see what bearing the matter would have on my willingness to get out of here and to help others do so,' he replied icily.

'Good for you Green. I can see that we will get on! I don't give a damn about your home life and, in any case, it's none of my bloody business.' Bushell roared with laughter and slapped Green on the back. 'Relax and I'll make you a brew.'

There was only one subject that would change Bushell's mood from warm bonhomie to an icy chill that affected everyone in the room.

He hated all Germans with an equal loathing, no matter who they were. It hadn't always been so. He had escaped to Prague and been hidden by a Czech family. Then Heydrich[1] had been killed by the Resistance, fatally poisoned by the horsehair stuffing of his car seat that had been blasted into his body by the explosion that had been set to kill him. There was a crackdown on all Czechs friendly to the Allies. Bushell was warned to flee, and the whole family had been killed by the Gestapo for hiding him. He would never forget or forgive them for this, and he redoubled his already formidable efforts to escape.

'There is an escape under way at the moment. Two chaps[2] are digging a tunnel under a wooden vaulting horse that is taken out each day and placed in exactly the same spot. I won't tell you their names at the moment because there is really no reason for you to know them. Soon they will have dug under the wire and they have a very good chance of getting out. We shall call on you to help in some way in due course,' said Bushell.

They drank their hot tea from Klim[3] tins with soldered handles. Soon after, Green and Dodge left at different times and walked back to their huts by different routes.

It was the summer of 1943. Quite a lot had happened at home in the previous year. Catherine had married Clive, her Army officer, before his posting to India. Someone in his regiment must have had a sense of humour, thought Green. Adrian had stood in for him at the wedding and had given his sister away. He was now due to go back to OCTU for another determined bash at a commission. London had been heavily bombed over a long period of time. The Baedecker raids[4] had given way to regular pounding of Britain's major cities.

It was a warm summer with glorious skies. Great towers of rising clouds swelled above the monotony of the rows of pine trees. Green ached to be out of the camp.

In the autumn a remarkable thing happened. Three men, not two, got out of the tunnel that had been built under the wooden horse. The two tunnellers, Williams and Codner, had been joined at the last minute by Philpot. All three men were clear of Sagan and had a very good chance of making it back home.

Green knew Oliver Philpot. He had met him at Radley when Adrian was there. Philpot was a loner, a quiet, determined man who relied on himself more than on anyone else. He undoubtedly would have struck out on his own when clear of the tunnel. He reminded Green of Bushell in one of his darker moods – not always easy to live with but absolutely vital to the war effort.

Immediately after the escape, everyone was locked into their huts, while goons and ferrets[5] in their blue boiler suits searched every bit of the camp. Their heavy boots could be heard clumping across the roof, accompanied by shouts of 'Fall off, Fritz' and other less polite messages relating not only to their future well-being but also to their dubious origins. Ferrets climbed around in the roof spaces and wormed around under the huts, probing, poking and measuring. At last someone found the far end of the tunnel outside the wire and some hapless Gefreiter[6] was ordered to crawl in with a torch. He emerged several minutes later, grimy but relieved, in the middle of the sports ground.

Senior German officers shouted themselves hoarse, as did senior German NCOs. Repeated and prolonged Appels were held, with bored guards supervising bored officers. There was a new feeling in the air that no amount of bullying could quash. Escapes were possible, and men could get home.

More Allied airmen were being purged to the camp straight from Dulag. The news was generally good; it seemed that the tide of the war was beginning to turn against the Nazis. The Russians were gradually advancing from the east, the bombing of German cities and industries was happening on a regular basis and the war in the desert had turned firmly in the Allies' favour some time ago.

Back in the summer of 1942 the East Compound had become too crowded with airmen of all nations. The Germans had to do something. A group of the older inhabitants were told at an hour's notice that they were being purged. They collected their kit and paraded on the sports ground for the last time. They were then marched out of the compound in small groups to the railway station. Green was pleased to see that Dodge was in his detail. Dodge was not his usual relaxed self; Green was certain that he was about to 'try something'. He had always been a gambler and had not had the chance for some time to make a break for freedom.

Sitting for long hours in the dusty station made the men bored and fidgety. Green appreciated the change of scene. Nobody knew where they were going; hopefully they would go in a westerly direction.

It was a bit of a shock when the long train onto which they were crammed appeared to be heading in a north-easterly direction. Green was glad that they would possibly be closer to the sea. It was now obvious that they were crossing into Poland. Green hoped he would not end up back in Stalag Luft II.

In the middle of the night a thump and the sound of smashing glass was accompanied by two shots and loud shouts and curses in German. Someone had jumped from the train. Green would bet his last dollar that it was Dodge, as the train squealed to a halt. In the morning he was proved to have been right. As the train arrived at a long weed-grown platform on the edge of the small Polish town of Schubin, a large armed guard stood tensely in front of the boarded-up station building.

The prisoners were prodded onto the platform and made to form up in fives. Appel was taken, and the column was marched off down a long road past hayfields and isolated farmhouses to the inevitable high barbed-wire gates and striped sentry box. This camp was a small one and was called Offlag XXIB.[7]

Green was glad to see many people he knew arriving at the camp. 'Wings' Day was here, Carr and even Dickens from Marlow. There was no sign of Dodge; Green hoped that he was now on the way home. Life soon settled down to the old routine; Green was soon in demand for his bread and butter puddings once again. He was glad to see proper trees outside the wire, trees that reflected the changing seasons: oak, ash and silver birch.

One morning Appel stretched on interminably. A vehicle could be heard approaching the main gate. With a grinding of gears, it was admitted into the main compound. Four heavily armed and steel-helmeted soldiers pushed a tall moustached man out of the back of a truck. He landed nimbly and was marched, hands high in the air, in front of the assembled airmen towards the cooler. It was the Dodger, looking none the worse for his few days of freedom.

The Senior British Officer called the parade to attention. Dozens of heels smacked the ground at exactly the same time. Just before he disappeared into the cooler, Dodge grinned widely and spread the two fingers of each upraised hand in the victory sign. The officers stood to attention for two long minutes, each man staring resolutely ahead. Then a firm voice called them to stand at ease and then to stand easy.

The Germans fought to control themselves. Only the commandant remained icily aloof. Every minute of the two hours that the prisoners stood in the open was worth it. Cool breezes blew across them and bird-song floated up from the woods below. Above all, the Germans were forced to stand there too, waiting for word of dismissal from the commandant.

Dodge showed up in the compound three weeks later looking fit and rested. He saw the whole thing as a joke, a way to let off steam before the really serious escape was fully planned. He had pushed out a lavatory window in the train and jumped before his guard had a chance to stop him. One of the ensuing shots had come a bit close for comfort. He had landed in a ditch and lay winded while the train passed him, before the brakes were hurriedly applied and the train brought to a standstill several hundred yards away.

Eventually he picked himself up and crawled away into the darkness. The sight of a muddy man in full daylight was too much for the local police, who arrested Dodge and handed him over once more to the Germans. 'Next time', thought a bedraggled Dodge, 'will be the last time. It will be for real.'

A few weeks later a new tunnel was started. Green helped to disperse the soil by shuffling around like a penguin balancing an egg on its feet. He noticed that every time a German came into the compound, the man was covertly followed and observed by stooges, who recorded all times and movements. The eventful autumn wore on with beautiful clouds in the sky and real progress below ground.

Green knew that this was the largest and best-organised escape so far. He knew that 'Wings' Day was involved and that a large number of airmen as well as Dodge were planning to get out through the tunnel and hightail it for home. It was not his turn to escape, but he was more than glad to help with the soil dispersal. He knew that other men with no hope of escape were busy forging documents, altering uniforms to civilian clothes and copying maps. All these activities gave purpose to camp life and put a spring back in the step of many of the prisoners.

In the meantime camp thespian productions continued. Plays were adapted and rehearsed, lines learned and costumes made. A lot of clandestine activity went on behind the scenes with the tools and materials supplied for costumes and scenery. The constant rehearsal of songs, often led by Dodge with great enthusiasm, covered the sounds of sawing and hammering from the covert workshops producing shoring for the tunnel.

At last the time for breaking out arrived. There was a tension in the camp that must have been apparent to the Germans. They had no way of finding anything out without making fools of themselves, so they maintained a sullen and watchful silence. It was hard to hide the absence of thirty-four officers at morning Appel, so the hue and cry was on. Endless parades in the weak sunlight accompanied by shouting Germans and growling dogs alternated with long stifling confinements in gloomy huts. Tempers frayed on both sides.

Then tired and tattered men in civilian clothes were returned in small groups to the camp over a period of several days. The first men back went straight into the cooler before they had a chance to tell any of their comrades where they had been or what they had done.

Soon the cooler was full to bursting point and solitary confinement was a thing of the past. Ferrets in their boiler suits climbed over and under huts. They probed everywhere they could with their long iron rods hoping to find evidence of forgery, mapping and other skulduggery. They found next to nothing, and their sour mood deepened. With all prisoners returned to camp, some men were sent straight back to their huts, where they entertained their mess mates with all the details of their escapes. They posted stooges at strategic places round the huts to make sure that no enemy ears could hear their tales. 'Wings' Day came out of the cooler more determined and hawk-like than ever, a silent and brooding presence whose time had not yet come. Green could not help thinking that the stakes for the prisoners were now higher than they had ever been.

Before any further escape plans could be formulated, a large group of officers was purged back to Stalag Luft III just over the border in Germany. Green and Dodge were among the group who took over the new North Compound at Sagan.[8] They found new huts and a spacious compound, where they mixed with Americans and airmen from all the Allied nations.

Green saw this move as a positive thing. The Russians were beating back the Nazis after the terrible Stalingrad campaign. It was only a matter of time before they were swarming into Poland and wreaking their revenge on Germany. He decided to double up on his study of the Russian language. Hopefully he would not be around when the troops arrived with snow on their boots.

The mournful pine forest that surrounded the camp stretched away to the south and east. There was no variation in the foliage from one year's end to another. Green decided that he disliked pine trees. It was time to get out.

The first few days at Sagan were spent re-establishing contact with friends. Bushell was back with a new glint in his eye, a new grim determination in his sometimes dour expression. He began to collect men who would be indispensable to a major escape. There were a number of Americans he knew he could depend on; George Harsh was one. Bushell wanted to involve as many characters as desperate as himself.

Soon Green and Dodge moved into a small room in Hut 104. They got on well and were much older than the vast majority of the other officers. They were fairly comfortable in the new compound. But they never forgot why they were there; escape was in the air.

They found the commandant, Colonel von Lindeiner-Wildau,[9] to be a fair and compassionate man. He was remote and strict but respected his officer inmates. Many of them developed a respect for him and even a grudging liking. He had served with distinction in the First World War, had been wounded three times and been awarded the iron cross twice. To him the officers in his charge were gentlemen first and foremost; when his patience occasionally gave way, it was more in sorrow than in anger. Green suspected that he considered Hitler a trumped-up and hysterical little junior NCO.

At Appel von Lindeiner was always immaculately turned out and always on time. He did not like to waste time and did not expect his charges to do so. More than once he hinted to the Senior British Officer that the airmen would be much better off in his charge than as guests of the Gestapo or Kripo.[10] He genuinely believed in the futility of escape and tried to make his prisoners as comfortable as possible. He provided sports equipment and a good library. He used the cooler sparingly.

Of course, he thwarted as many escape plans as he could. His second in command and intelligence officer, Major Broili,[11] was a cultured and friendly man who spoke several languages and left the shouting and hard-man stuff to the senior NCOs. The third in command, Hauptmann Pieber,[12] tried to be a friend to everyone. He was genuinely charming most of the time but was considered slippery by those who disliked him. But he did try his hardest to get along with everyone, an impossible task in a POW camp.

Von Lindeiner had a point. Conditions were better in Stalag Luft III than in most other camps. It was a battle of wills; a few words with Bushell, and the majority of the officers who were thinking of settling down in relative comfort to sit out the rest of the war would probably think again. Green had never thought of staying put and needed no convincing that his duty lay in continuing to help all escape attempts that were going on. It mattered little to him if he himself were to be given a chance to get out or not. At his age, he doubted if he would be chosen as an active escaper. The only time he ever lost his temper was when it was suggested that he should sit back and leave the dirty and dangerous work to others. He surprised himself and the man to whom he was talking with the coarseness of his language and the vehemence of his expression. He apologised to the officer, but knew that he had firmly put his case. Both Bushell and Dodge were highly amused by his outburst, but were too sensible ever to refer to it. It reinforced the fact that Green was a valuable ally whom they probably wouldn't ask to dig the tunnel but who would quietly help the escape effort in any way he could, however hard or tedious.

In the summer of 1943 Green found himself summoned to a meeting with Bushell. He knew what was coming and was happy to report to the senior officer.

'Sit down Green. I'm sure you know what is going on under this compound. There are three tunnels[13] at the moment, each with a good chance of getting under the wire sometime in the New Year. We know that the Russians are coming and we want to disrupt the German war effort in every way we can. We plan to get a large number of chaps out all at the same time. Some have a chance of a home run; most will tie up valuable enemy resources for a long time. There is a lot of risk involved; a number of us have been told that if we escape again we will be shot.

This is meant to discourage us, but we have to go ahead. We cannot just sit here on our fat arses and let everyone else liberate us one day.'

'We are going to win the war. The tide is turning. Often we can see big raids on Berlin. The increased number of officers coming into this camp is a reflection of the greater number of raids on German cities. The Americans are doing great work and a lot are turning up here too.'

'I would like you to help us. The job of a penguin is tedious and dirty but vitally necessary to our plan. There is a slim chance that your name could be chosen as an escaper. You have a perfect right to decline either job. Nobody will think less of you if you decide just to sit tight. But I don't think that you're that kind of man. I'll give you twenty-four hours to think it over.'

Green smiled briefly.

'I can give you my answer right now if you wish.' He paused mischievously. 'What do you think I'm going to tell you?'

Bushell stared at him, his icy eyes boring into Green's soul. Green waited, amused by Bushell's intensity.

'Of course I'll help with the earth. And, if given the chance, I'll be through that tunnel with the rest of them. You can count on that.'

A large grin spread over Bushell's dour features. He stood up and clapped Green on the back.

'I never doubted you. I'm delighted that you want to join us.'

He reached into his locker and produced a bottle of cloudy raisin hooch and poured two generous measures into two Klim tins. The drink tasted of boot polish and sheep's urine but warmed Green's heart.

'Had you hesitated I would have said, "As the oldest prisoner in the camp you are entitled to your peace and quiet. You have done enough and have earned it."'

'And I would have told you to stick those words up your twisted lawyer's arse,' replied Green.

Green left the room a few minutes later, feeling slightly the worse for wear. He had a new tendency to list to port and decided to stay off the hooch in future.

As he lay on his bunk, he thought about the coming weeks and months. The grey Silesian winter was coming soon, with its icy winds and desperately low temperatures. The impenetrable pine trees just outside the wire seemed to mock him, telling him that, like the view, nothing would ever change. The work ahead would be tedious and risky. There would be no glamour in it, nothing heroic, just the slog of shifting heavy bags of intractable yellow sand while the exhausting and tedious digging went on below the surface. The three tunnels, Tom, Dick and Harry, were sophisticated and well engineered. They went down over 30 feet before heading for the flat land beyond the wire. As yet Green did not know where they were. He would be told when he needed to know. In the meantime he would carry his two bags of sand and place them where they would not be detected.

That autumn the sand ended up in hastily dug gardens and in the roofs of huts. Somewhere else would have to be found in the winter, when thick snow covered the bumpy ground. Green grew used to filthy trousers and gritty socks. Fortunately his blanket covered his grotesquely baggy trousers with their internal bags. He often felt like an ancient Charlie Chaplin shuffling around leaking sand over his boots and treading it into the earth. He felt like a man with a permanent state of gritty incontinence.

Winter arrived, and most of the escaping activities were forced to close down. The forging of papers and passes continued during the short hours of comparative daylight. This department was known as 'Dean and Dawson', after the well-known firm of travel agents in London's West End. Civilian clothes continued to be adapted from various items of uniform. Fleet Air Arm trousers were particularly popular. Their relative scarcity made them less familiar to the Germans. Buttons and badges were removed from tunics and greatcoats, and dyes were concocted from tea, boot polish and even the covers of books removed from the library.

The thought of escape made the dark winter months bearable. Green had now spent over three and a half years in captivity. His son, Adrian, was now a subaltern in the newly formed Reconnaissance Corps. His daughter, Catherine, had now been married for eighteen months; Green had heard all about it several months after the event. Catherine's husband, Clive, a lieutenant in the Hampshires, was supervising the building of airstrips in India. At least he would be fairly safe there, although he had never been able to stand hot weather.

Green wondered how his wife was back in Bourne End. He felt that she resented the fact that he had joined up and then been shot down. He knew that she was glad that he was alive but also knew that life would not be easy back in Wharf Lane.

He knew that he had been a disappointment to her. He should have been running the family paper mill in Wooburn Green. He should have continued to be one of the managers. In the 1920s his brother-in-law, who had been busy feathering his nest while Green was doing quite the opposite in the trenches, had started to gain control of the mill.[14] Green had rightly opposed the shift in power, but had been outvoted and had become senior sales representative. He was secretly happier travelling all over northern Europe buying raw materials and selling the finished product. He knew he was not a businessman and lacked the crass ambition needed to manage the firm. What rankled with him was the unfairness of the takeover – a Yorkshire pipsqueak had taken from him his rightful inheritance.

So here he was in Silesia. When he returned home, he would cut loose from the mill and set up some kind of business elsewhere. In a way he was still master of his own destiny. He smiled to himself; 'Triumph of the Will' was the answer in Nazi terms.[15] The film director Leni Riefenstahl had a point: if you wanted something hard enough, you could make it happen. Morals would play a part here. He would not behave as selfishly as his brother-in-law. He would cut loose and hurt no one. There was a parallel in his present condition. If he were to escape, it would not be at the expense of any of his brother officers.

Enough of the 'Mill Row'; some things were best dusted off and then forgotten. The future was what counted; Green must get himself out of Stalag Luft III if humanly possible. If necessary, he was prepared to die in the attempt. He was not a selfish man; he would love to see his son and daughter again back in England. He had accepted a lot in his life and was still fighting. He derived much comfort from his friend Evelyn's regular letters. She was able to understand what his life had become.

During the cold, dark winter of 1943 a new place was found for the distribution of sand from the tunnels. Seat number thirteen in the new camp theatre lifted to reveal a huge space below. Tons of sand could be poured into this triangular void without compromising anything. Green and his fellow penguins could take a great interest in the thespian arts and dump their diurnal loads under the rising ranks of seats every evening.

Green was fortunate in having a genuine interest in the theatre. He was no actor but thoroughly enjoyed the rehearsals he attended every evening in his recently acquired capacious Polish greatcoat. He relieved himself nightly of his sandy burden and became very familiar with the workings of seat number thirteen.

One dark evening Green was shuffling over to the theatre when the skirt of his coat snagged on one of the pickets holding up the warning wire a few yards inside the perimeter. The jerk to his hand released half a bag of sand onto the frozen snow of the path. Green watched with horror as the sand trickled onto the snow. He stamped his feet and flung his arms above his head in a Highland Fling. The guards in the two towers nearby laughed as the ridiculous figure in the oversized coat danced around to the skirl of imaginary pipes. After a frantic dance, Green solemnly bowed in turn to both towers and continued his walk to the theatre with beating heart and a feeling of accomplishment.

One day, back in the summer, one of the tunnels had been discovered by the ferrets. There was the usual hue and cry, the usual lengthy Appels in the dust. No one was found missing, and the usual searches yielded little of value. Bushell remarked grimly that the other two tunnels were now even more important and that Jerry would probably rest on his laurels for a while. He redoubled his theatrical efforts to convince the Germans that he no longer had escape on his mind.

It was finally decided to concentrate tunnelling efforts on Harry. The entrance to this deep tunnel was in Hut 104 in the end room next door to the small room shared by Green and Dodge. Dick would be used for storage and as an underground workshop. With the heavy onset of winter, the digging of tunnels had to stop, but plans continued unceasingly.

Green wrote his regular letters home. He wrote mostly to Adrian, to Evelyn and sometimes to Catherine and Dorothea. He emphasised the fact that he was fit and well and hoped that the war would be over soon. He told them about the plays that were being produced and the books he was reading. He described the skies and sunsets and his daily walks around the inside of the perimeter of the camp. He thanked them for the letters and parcels they regularly sent and gave the impression to the censors that he had settled down to a long and comfortable captivity as a guest of the Third Reich.

He continued to study the Russian language. He was most amused by a sketch by a fellow officer of him studying and smoking a Woodbine.[16] He even sent it home to Adrian to show him that he hadn't changed much since he had been 'in the bag'. From time to time representatives of the Red Cross took photos of groups of men in the camp. They posed looking tough, serious and resolute, as if the camp were a piece of cake. The unposed pictures were more revealing; one showed Green as a lonely figure in the snow against the stark wire. He still looked tough but also curiously vulnerable in his dark glasses and ragged clothes. He looked like a man who should have been sitting in front of a warm fire in his snug home in the Thames Valley. The irony of this photograph was not lost on those who knew him.

One evening he was talking to Johnny Dodge in their room in Hut 104. Dodge was cheerful and ebullient and Green was his usual quiet and rather withdrawn self.

'I remember you rather differently from 1916,' said Dodge hesitantly.

'Yes, I suppose I was more outgoing back then,' replied Green, conscious of the fact the Dodge had put his finger on what he would not usually have admitted was his problem.

'You were more extrovert back then, with your terrible puns and awful jokes. You don't have to tell me what happened if you don't want to. I won't be offended if you don't.'

'I haven't really thought about it. The terrible puns have got worse, if anything. I don't mind telling you at all, however. I was always naturally quiet but with noisy interludes. After the Somme I must have changed, become grimmer and harder to live with. It was the waste that got to me. The men I was responsible for were decimated; some of them just vanished into the mud and were never seen again. Men I knew well were blown apart, shot, gassed, and I could do nothing to save them. I used to think that by being a good officer I could care for them and somehow keep them safe. I found that I could no more do that than fly in the air. The worst part was losing men that I had thoroughly disliked. I felt even more guilty when that happened.'

'The men used to call me "Fat Aunty"; not to my face of course. I took it as a compliment. I cared very much about them, their safety. Even behind the lines I used to worry about the ones who got the clap. I was probably harder on the men I liked than the others.'

'It was during the Somme offensive that I realised that I was losing my faith. It had been so important to me and then it was gone. I was no longer able to pray and I felt abandoned. How can one feel abandoned by something that doesn't exist? That's a thorny theological question.'

'In the winter of 1916 I was home on leave. I was due to be married on my birthday, just before Christmas. I thought that I was the luckiest man in the world, but even so I had misgivings. My future wife was a lovely and a wonderful girl. But did I deserve her?'

'The day before the wedding I was walking home from Marlow. It was a crisp, frosty morning and I strode along in the Bourne End direction. I had passed the pub at the turning to Little Marlow and had walked on for about a mile when something stopped me in my tracks. I turned and looked at a hand-painted sign on the other side of the road. It said: "No road beyond the cemetery."'

'That's exactly it!" I thought. I took great comfort from the starkness of that sign. It summed up what my life had become. No longer could I pretend that I would take holy orders. I had been changed, and there was no way back. The truth as I now saw it was entirely apparent to me and I could relax. On that day I shrugged an enormous burden from my shoulders. The years at Cambridge seemed a long time away and the future was very uncertain.'

'I paid a price for that decision. I became withdrawn and quiet and I must have been hard to live with. I feel sorry for Dorothea. She is full of life and of high expectations. I must be a great disappointment to her but I just can't help it.'

'I understand what you must have gone through, Bernard, and I value what you have told me. But were you ever afraid at any point in the trenches?'

'I was terrified a lot of the time but I couldn't let it show. I had to lead the men and show them a good example. If I had cracked once, I could never have continued, and once I realised that God had not abandoned us, I found comfort in that. It is easier to believe that there is no God than to believe that God turned his back on us.'

'I found that I could function in situations of great stress. It was just a chance thing that happened; all the fear would lift off when there was fighting to be done. But it came at a price. The detachment that took me over remained deep within me. I found that it was the everyday things that found me wanting.'

'I'll give you an example: when Catherine caught the train home from school in High Wycombe I would meet her at the station in Bourne End and walk back with her to our house in Wharf Lane. I was always delighted to see her but could never find anything to say to her as we walked those familiar few hundred yards to the house. I don't know what she must have thought of me at the time. I was the same with Dorothea, almost silent, as if I had nothing to say, nothing to offer. No wonder she must feel that I am a big disappointment. It seems that I am no longer capable of communication with the people close to me, the people I love.'

'I understand what you are telling me. You never had a chance to talk about what happened in the last war. You kept it all locked up inside yourself. Many men have done that. Thank you for telling me this; of course it will go no further.'

'I really haven't talked about it at all. In fact I haven't spoken so much for a very long time. I could talk about the Somme and Ypres until the cows come home but I'm sure that nobody would be in the slightest bit interested. But I feel better for unburdening some of this baggage and I thank you for showing an interest.'

Dodge leaned back on his crate.

'I found that the war made me slightly crazy and more extrovert. That's the way it took me, I guess. I couldn't take it too seriously or I'd go mad. So I went into politics, unsuccessfully as it turned out, and travelled all over the world getting into outlandish scrapes. Here I am again back in prison camp pretending I'm a sane and responsible person yet knowing that really I'm not. It seems that I'm always trying to prove that I'm something I'm not.'

'You're more honest in your reaction to the horrors. I keep going back and prodding them to see what will happen. I can't leave it alone. The "forthcoming event" is very important to me. I have to succeed at something to prove to myself that I am not just a restless bloody fool.'

'Let's get back to this tomorrow. I must mug up on the Cyrillic alphabet and get it straight in my head so that I can greet our Soviet liberators when the time comes and they arrive at the camp gate with snow on their boots. Thanks for raising the question of the Great War; it helps to explain why we're here in this place right now.'

As the bitter winter grew colder and bleaker the two men spent much time in the evenings talking about the First World War. They came to realise that things really were simpler in the present war. They really were fighting a just war, resisting the influence of a mad tyrant who had set out to inflict his psychoses on the whole world. He had to be stopped at any cost.

Often the men would talk in the darkness when the lights would flicker and dim and go out. They would not bother to light a candle stub but would wrap their coarse Polish blankets tighter around themselves for warmth. They felt suspended in a sea of unreality yet strangely free, removed from the camp to a world of the past that was infinitely worse. Green found the conversations exhausting but liberating. Some evenings he had to force himself to continue, and Dodge respected the effort it cost him. Occasionally they would agree not to talk on certain evenings, usually when dull explosions and the hint of flickering searchlights in the north suggested a large bombing raid on Berlin. The two men would lie in the darkness and think of the damage being delivered to the Nazi war machine. They would also think of the civilians huddling terrified beneath the bombs raining down on their blocks of flats and houses from above.

The days were bright and very cold, the wind coming almost unimpeded from Siberia. The trees wore their mantles of snow for months on end, and the forest seemed dead. Trees cracked with the frost and split to the ground. The tired sentries stamped their way round the outside of the fence, trying desperately to keep warm and stay semi-alert. Some of the veterans of the Eastern Front remembered the Russian cold penetrating their inadequate clothing. They remembered frostbite and sentries freezing to death at their posts, slipping away from the awful icy cold to a merciful oblivion. A few remembered eating the frozen flesh of their dead comrades in order to prolong an existence that was becoming as agonising as the icy inner circle of hell. These men still felt happy to be where they were in the Fatherland, with the end of their ordeal a finite number of minutes away. Quite a number were beginning to realise that the Thousand Year Reich was also coming to an end. They dreaded the coming of the Russian army above anything else and trusted their fates to the British and the Americans above all else.

Suddenly the commandant of the camp dealt a very serious blow to

A slightly scruffy Bernard Green at Trinity College, Cambridge, 1910. (Jason Warr)

Recently commissioned Second Lieutenant Green before being assigned to the Ox and Bucks Light Infantry, autumn 1914. (Jennifer Green)

Lieutenant Green (with hair), Ox and Bucks Light Infantry 1914. (Jennifer Green)

Lieutenant Green, Ox and Bucks Light Infantry, 1915. The 'T' collar dog indicates service in the Territorial Army. (Catherine Buckmaster)

Lieutenant Green, back middle, with brother officers in France, 1915. (Jason Warr)

Lieutenant Green, front, third from left, Ox and Bucks Light Infantry, Ypres, Belgium, 1915. (Jason Warr)

Kathleen Dorothea Connell before her marriage to Bernard Green in 1916. (Catherine Buckmaster)

Captain Green, seated, seconded to the Machine Gun Corps, in an informal postcard photograph taken on the Somme in 1916. Note the combination of officers' ranks on the shoulder strap and lower sleeve. (Jason Warr)

Captain Green, back centre, MGC, the Somme, 1916. The lieutenant with the stick in the front row is wearing the ribbon of the Military Cross. (Jason Warr)

Major Green with his son Adrian and his father Roland Green, Bourne End, 1920. (Laurence Green)

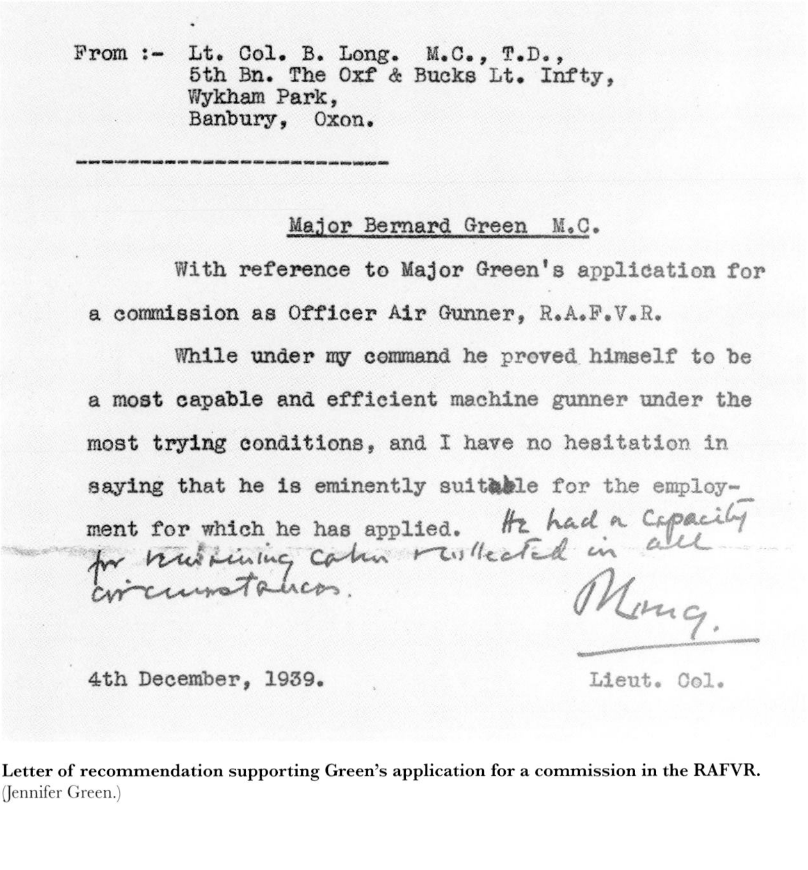

From :- Lt. Col. B. Long. M.C., T.D.,
5th Bn. The Oxf & Bucks Lt. Infty,
Wykham Park,
Banbury, Oxon.

Major Bernard Green M.C.

With reference to Major Green's application for a commission as Officer Air Gunner, R.A.F.V.R.

While under my command he proved himself to be a most capable and efficient machine gunner under the most trying conditions, and I have no hesitation in saying that he is eminently suitable for the employment for which he has applied. He had a capacity for maintaining calm & collected in all circumstances.

B Long.

4th December, 1939. Lieut. Col.

Letter of recommendation supporting Green's application for a commission in the RAFVR. (Jennifer Green.)

Officer Cadet Green, middle, fourth from left, at the beginning of the aerial gunnery course at RAF Aldergrove, autumn 1939. (Jason Warr)

Officer Cadet Green during aerial gunnery training at RAF Aldergrove, Northern Ireland, spring 1940. (Jennifer Green)

Pilot Officer on Probation Green, front centre, at completion of the course, RAF Aldergrove, spring 1940. (Jason Warr)

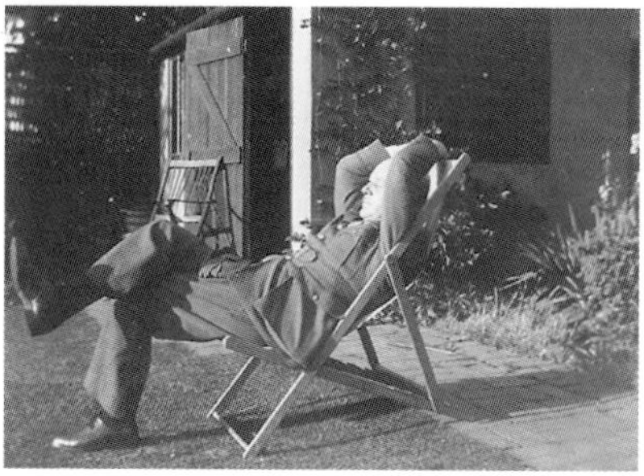

Pilot Officer on Probation Bernard Green at home in the back garden of Cortegar, Wharf Lane, Bourne End, Bucks, on leave in May 1940. He was on the point of leaving home for 44 Squadron at RAF Waddington in Lincolnshire. (Jennifer Green)

Hampden Mark 1 L4087 on the beach at Kandestederne, Denmark, after being stripped of everything useful by the Germans. (Bangsbo Museum, Denmark)

Pilot Officer Green, seated middle, with friends at Stalag I, Barth, in 1941. (Jason Warr)

Pilot Officer Green, fourth from right, Stalag Luft I, Barth, 1941. (Jason Warr)

Flying Officer Green, right, with friends at Offlag XXIB, Schubin, Poland, in 1942. This photograph was probably taken by Hauptmann Hans Pieber. (Jason Warr)

Flight Lieutenant Green walking with Major 'Johnny' Dodge in the recently cleared North Compound of Stalag Luft III, Sagan, in the summer of 1943. (Jason Warr)

Hut 104 on the night of the Great Escape. Bernard Green sitting at the end of the bunk on the right. (Jimmy James archive)

A lone Flight Lieutenant Green, North Compound, Stalag Luft III, Sagan, winter 1943/44. (Jennifer Green)

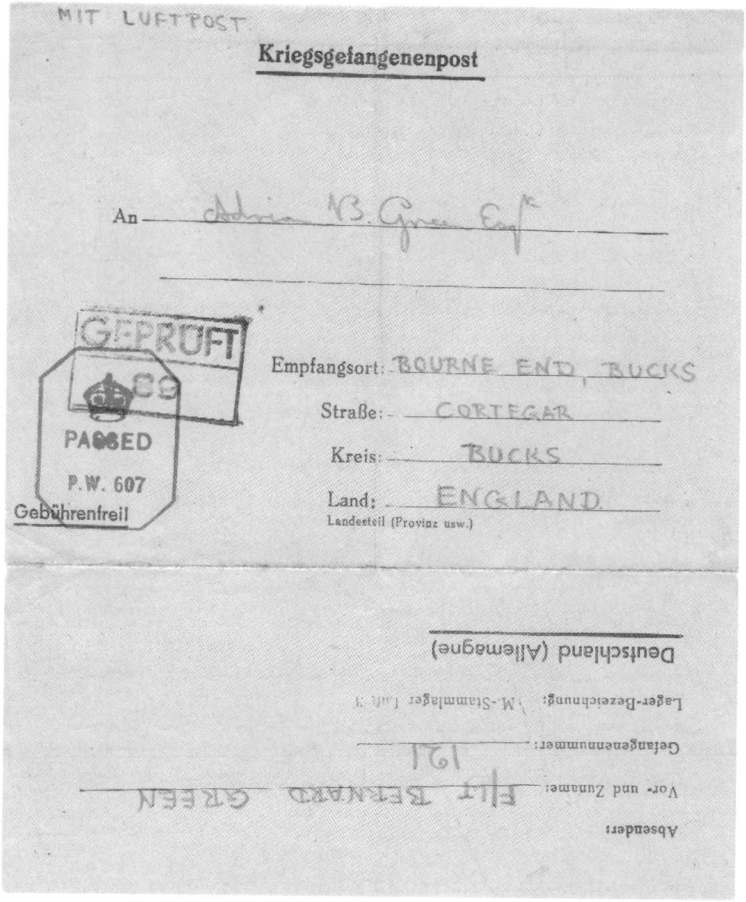
MIT LUFTPOST

Kriegsgefangenenpost

An Adrian B. Green Esq

GEPRÜFT 89

PASSED P.W. 607

Gebührenfrei!

Empfangsort: BOURNE END, BUCKS

Straße: CORTEGAR

Kreis: BUCKS

Land: ENGLAND

Landesteil (Provinz usw.)

Deutschland (Allemagne)

Lager-Bezeichnung: M.-Stammlager Luft 3

Gefangenennummer: 191

Vor- und Zuname: F/Lt BERNARD GREEN

Absender:

Bernard Green wrote numerous letters and postcards to his son Adrian while in captivity. This letter was written after the Great Escape and Bernard states: 'I have certainly been more fortunate than the commandant of our special police though it has come to much the same in the end.' Possibly this is a reference to the murder of Roger Bushell. A full transcript of all the letters can be found in Appendix 6 (Laurence Green)

My dear A, Very many thanks for yours (25/4/44) of 5/12, 12/12, & 7/1. Please wish your mother very many happies of 7/5 from me. Yes, I can imagine Clive's lockers! hope he's OK now, give him my paternal blessing if you're writing. Am now in a room with chap called Mackintosh - one of the leading lights of the theatre - he gave masterly interpretation of "Higgins" in Pygmalion - is tall with long untidy hair (off the stage!) - told him it was a pity you weren't here in my place! our room has frieze of all the posters of plays since theatre opened. Yes, I'm pretty well sure it was Stan - strongly built - medium height - fair. Am thinking of you more than usual these days, wondering what you will be up to. Congrats to Jim. I understand there may be a good chance of Thelma meeting her husband. Hear very good accounts of your health - keep it up! am also very fit. I have certainly been more fortunate than the commandant of our special police though it has come to much the same in the end - do you remember his talk in the cinema at Malor? I wonder where you will be when you get this letter. Every blessing - BG

THE ROYAL AIR FORCES ASSOCIATION

AND

THE R.A.F. ESCAPING SOCIETY

Announce

WORLD PREMIERE

"THE GREAT ESCAPE"

A United Artists Corporation release of the Mirisch-Alpha Production of Paul Brickhill's True Story of the Mass Escape from Stalag Luft III

Starring

STEVE McQUEEN
JAMES GARNER
RICHARD ATTENBOROUGH
JAMES DONALD
DONALD PLEASENCE
JOHN LEYTON

To be held at

THE ODEON, LEICESTER SQUARE, W.C.

(by the generosity of THE RANK ORGANISATION)

Thursday, 20th June, 1963

ALL PROCEEDS TO R.A.F. CHARITIES

Bernard Green and his wife Evelyn attended the premiere of *The Great Escape*. He remarked that his seat number should have been no.13. (Jason Warr)

Programme of the world charity premiere of the film *The Great Escape* shown on 20 June 1963.
(Jason Warr)

Green's medals from both wars. From left to right: Military Cross, 1914–15 Star, 1916–18 War Medal, 1919 Victory Medal with MiD oak leaf spray, 1939–45 Star, Air Crew Europe Star, 1939–45 War Medal with MiD oak leaf spray, Special Constabulary Medal for long service (1926–39).
(Contributed anonymously)

the plans for mass escape. Colonel von Lindeiner announced at morning Appel that all the American prisoners were to be transferred to the new South Compound.[17] Green thought that this would happen soon; on his daily walks round the perimeter he had seen the Russian prisoners nearing the completion of the work.

The trouble with the move was that several key players in the escape organisation would suddenly disappear. George Harsh,[18] a wild and incisive American, was in charge of security. He posted stooges and managed the extremely complex system of observing the enemy within the camp. He had been there from the beginning and had enabled the whole scheme to move forward. He would be sorely missed, as would all the other American officers, who had bonded well with nearly everyone and contributed much more to the escape effort than their numbers indicated.

Green was afraid that Dodge would be forced to move to the South Compound as well.

'Not bloody likely!' said Dodge. 'I became a British citizen years ago before I went into politics. Most of the squareheads who run this camp couldn't tell a British accent from a Bronx cheer,[19] old chap.' He said this in the most expertly delivered clipped English accent, which caused Green to chuckle.

Soon the Americans had reluctantly departed with all their kit and, for a few days, the camp was a quieter and a sadder place. Bushell and his cadre soon replaced the vacant positions, and it was business as usual – as much as the freezing winter weather allowed.

Green continued his endless perambulations of the inside of the wire. He was often alone and walked as fast as his old heel wound allowed. In cold weather it would begin to ache and remind him of Ypres. Perhaps the wound had done him a good turn; it had proved to be a 'blighty' one, and he was sent reluctantly home on 10 October 1918. Missing the last month of the war may have saved his life; by then he had had two wounds, which was rather tempting fate. He was paid £120 in compensation for his torn heel and promoted to the rank of Major. He was enabled to return to domestic life in Bourne End and start a family. In his heart of hearts he knew that the heel wound was slight compared to the change the war had wreaked to his very soul.

As he walked once again over the squeaky snow, he reflected on the number 2. The cold red orb of the sun sank slowly into the freezing pine forests casting long shadows through the stark wire. Green thought grimly: two wars, two wounds, two services, two adult children – one wife. He idly wondered how things would be when he eventually returned home permanently from a war for the second time.

His walk was interrupted by a red glow spreading from the north followed by the air-raid siren. He walked over to the nearest hut as the camp lights were switched off. With only the fading glow from the searchlights to guide him in the gathering dusk, he arrived at Hut 104 as he heard the baying of the hounds approaching from the Vorlager. Home and dry once again; it had been foolish to be out walking so late into the evening but never mind. A man had to be alone with his thoughts from time to time.

The tide of the war seemed to be turning even faster than before. This made the escape of even greater importance; it would not be good to fall into Russian hands, and who knew what the Germans would do in desperation as the Allies advanced into the Fatherland?

The work of the tunnel continued at an accelerated pace as winter dragged towards spring. Green and his fellow penguins moved tons of sand,[20] placing a lot of it under the floor of the theatre and in the hollow walls of some of the huts. The ferrets knew that something was up and watched with a suspicion bordering on the fanatical. Bushell threw himself into amateur dramatics as a blind, learning a major part as well as directing the many operations leading to the escape.

At last the time came for a day to be set for the mass breakout. The tunnel was now beyond the wire and would be beyond the tree line within a week. Spring was just over the horizon and the frost was apparently retreating. Bushell planned to spring 250 officers from the camp on a moonless night. A number of prisoners who had a good chance of getting home were to go through the tunnel first. They were the men who could speak German and French fluently and who had lived abroad. A number of them were Dutch, Norwegian and French. The others had to draw lots, and Green was delighted to be chosen to go. He would be among a party of men disguised as Czech wood mill workers, who would travel to Prague by train to meet up with members of the Czech Resistance. They were told that their chances of getting home were slim, and that, if they wished to remain in the camp, that they were at liberty to do so with no stain on their characters. Not a man turned down the offer of a dirty and dangerous journey through a deep and narrow tunnel shored up by bed boards[21] and a cold and uncertain flight through enemy country.

A number of men who had played a part in the escape preparations declined to take part in the lottery. Brickhill[22] knew that his claustrophobia would not let him even enter the deep dark hole hidden under the stove in the end room of Hut 104. He knew that his mind would snap as he lay sweating in the darkness of the tunnel 30 feet below the surface of the camp. He did not want to hold things up or endanger the lives of the men behind him, so he told Bushell that he could not do it.

Bushell shook him warmly by the hand and told him that it took true courage to admit one's own weakness. Brickhill came away feeling relieved and regretful in equal measure. He knew that Bushell himself had been warned that, if he escaped once more and was recaptured, he would probably be shot. Bushell himself had thought long and hard about the commandant's warning before deciding that one could only lead from the front. Von Lindeiner was not threatening him; he was just passing on what he had been told in the hope of keeping Bushell safe in his camp.

6. The Great Escape

The wet early spring came and went. Freezing fog and snow replaced the promise of better things. The tunnel was beyond the wire and the outside perimeter track. The moon was waning fast and the numerous documents had to be dated. The date of 24 March was chosen, because the moon would be tiny and low on the horizon, well below the tree line on that night.

On the day it snowed and froze hard. Former slush froze into ridges and an icy east wind blew all day; unsuitable weather for men in thin civilian clothes and travel passes stamped for that day and that day only. In the morning Green wrote a postcard to his son Adrian. He knew that it would take a long time to arrive. Adrian was serving as a lieutenant with the Reconnaissance Corps somewhere in the British Isles. Green hoped that Adrian was still up in Scotland, where he had been welcomed and had nearly married a Scots girl. In his card he stressed that he was well and in good spirits but that he was sick and tired of the snow and slush. He could say no more and hoped that this would be his last letter from Germany.

The day proceeded like any other day in captivity. After breakfast, Appel was held on the snowy parade ground. The officers tried to relax as much as possible, pretend that today was just the same as the hundreds of others spent in the bag. The count passed without incident, and the usual groups walked round the inside of the wire as normal.

The stooges stationed in doorways and windows were extra vigilant, as papers were finished and civilian clothes prepared. Bushell occupied himself with practising his lines for the forthcoming play. Anything that he hadn't foreseen or done was now too late. It was no good worrying about anything; just try to carry on as normal. There was a palpable air of tension as the day wore on. Some of the Germans sensed it and tried to find out what was happening. There were a few near misses as ferrets popped up here and there. Most treated it as a joke and engaged them in casual conversation.

'This war cannot last too much longer,' remarked Hauptmann Pieber to Green as he leaned against one of the huts.

'What will happen when the Russians or the British arrive at the gates of the camp?' replied Green.

'I think that you will tell them that we are not bad chaps and that we were not too hard on you,' said Pieber.

'You cannot win this war you know,' said Green.

'It is not our war. We did not want it and we are not all Nazis. We are loyal Germans who are fighting Communism and we do not hate you British.'

'Good luck,' replied Green as he turned away to resume his lonely walk round the inside of the wire. He liked Pieber as a man, just as he had great respect for von Lindeiner, the camp commandant. But he could not afford to be too obviously friendly. Walls had eyes and ears; Pieber could end up in deep trouble for what he had said to Green. The war effort must continue. The feelings of the captors could not be spared. Green realised that the Luftwaffe officers who ran the camp would become victims of the Nazis when the escape was discovered. He could not help the consequences.

Green took what he hoped would be his final walk around the camp in the afternoon. He walked alone and tried to fix in his mind the desolate study in black and white that was Stalag Luft III. The snow covered the ground in a thick blanket under which was a layer of ice. The weak sun would melt the top layer of snow, which would freeze as soon as the sun went below the tree line. Conditions were not ideal for escape, but the time had finally come…

As dusk fell, small groups of men, shrouded in greatcoats, converged on Hut 104. Other men moved off to different huts, where they would spend the night. Movements were made to seem as natural as usual, but there was a great element of risk in all the furtive scuttling. By the time the shutters were slammed from the outside and the dogs were released to roam the compound, there were nearly 200 men in the various rooms of Hut 104.

The stove in the end room was moved off its plinth and reconnected to its pipe so that the trap beneath it could be raised for the last time. The heat generated by the men squeezed into the hut made everyone sweat. Steam could be seen rising from the hut's poorly insulated walls. Strict silence was kept as men in civilian clothes sat and lay around waiting for full darkness and the word to go.

Green sat quietly on the end of a bunk not far from Dodge.[1] He was dressed as a workman in scruffy clothes, with a cloth cap and scarf hiding the remains of his RAF uniform. He had his papers and travel pass dated for the following day. He was pretending to be a Czech wood mill worker travelling to Prague with a group on leave.

Suddenly he started as a Wehrmacht corporal came into the room. He relaxed as he realised that it was Tobolski,[2] a Polish officer in disguise. Men sat and lay in the corridors as well as on all available surfaces. In the silence of the night they saw the shadows cast by the beams of the searchlights outside. Green thought of the cold, bored guards in their towers and marching round at the edge of the frigid woods. Soon he would be out there too, shivering but determined to put as much distance between himself and the camp as possible. He would have preferred a thaw and a warmer night, but would take as much advantage of the snow as he could. He realised that, once out of the tunnel, it would be every man for himself. Small groups of furtive men would attract attention to themselves. It would be lonely out there, he thought, as his stomach lurched at the thought of it.

Bushell moved among the men grinning and patting arms here and there. He appeared to have no nerves at all. Green knew otherwise and respected the man for his great courage. As ringleader, he was about to risk much more than anyone else. He would have it no other way; he was driven to escape, despite sensible thoughts to the contrary. His dark features encouraged all the men squeezed into the dark hut and gave out confidence and resolution.

The men had checked their kit and papers countless times. The tension was becoming unbearable for most. A few lay on beds or on the floor snoring peacefully. Green envied them their lack of imagination, as the fitful light from the searchlights momentarily blanched their sleeping faces.

At last the trapdoor was raised by its wires. It was heavy, and it took three straining men to place it silently on the floor beside the cooling stove. Green could not yet see the dark shaft yawning down 30 feet to the chamber at the tunnel's end.

A number of men moved among the recumbent shapes, indicating who was to go and when. The first escapers moved clumsily over legs and bodies towards the shaft. They were given a quick inspection before they climbed carefully down the shaft to the dimly lit tunnel below. Each gave the thumbs-up to Bushell as he vanished into the underworld. Green noticed that these first men were the best dressed of all and that some carried attaché cases. Soon Bushell was beckoned to the shaft, and Green would never forget his look of determination as he disappeared into the tunnel. It was a look that inspired Green to follow when his turn came, without a backward glance.

In the meantime there were delays. Soon men went down the hole every ten minutes instead of every two. Whispered messages told of blockages and falls of sand. Green waited as patiently as he could until his turn came in the small hours. Dodge had already gone when Green sat for a second on the edge of the shaft before climbing carefully down the wooden ladder to the chamber below.

The whole affair was a marvel of ingenuity. The shaft was lined by bed boards donated by almost every officer in the camp. A man sat at the bottom working a pump handle back and forth. A bellows made from two kitbags forced air through a valve into a pipeline made of Klim tins fitted together.[3] There was even electric light in the tunnel. Green's kit was checked once again, as he sat in the chamber at the bottom of the shaft. Gone was the smell of sweat and stale tobacco that had permeated the hut. At the tunnel's end it smelled of damp sand.

Green lowered himself onto a plank trolley, clutched his paper parcel to his chest and was off down the tunnel, pulled along a wooden railway by someone further down. He trundled slowly along, the wooden walls only inches from his face. A few bulges were apparent here and there. He tried to make sure that he did not snag any part of the walls or the roof.

He had been drawn a couple of hundred feet when the lights went out. He heard someone curse up ahead and was drawn on in the darkness until he came to a halt. A match was struck in front of his face and a fat lamp lit.

'It's probably a bloody air raid on Berlin,' a quiet voice spoke near his left ear. 'Don't worry; we'll soon have the lamps lit. Stay where you are for a minute.'

Green brought his arms back from in front of him and rested his head on them. He was fairly comfortable for the time being. He hoped he wouldn't have to spend hours in this position 30 feet below the frozen ground somewhere below the cooler.

He thought of Dorothea. He could hear her say: 'That's just the sort of thing that would happen to him, silly old fool…'

She had a point, he had to concede. Being stuck in the tunnel was the easy part. He was still part of a team. Soon he would be out on his own in a frozen landscape on the way to an occupied country where the Nazis had turned particularly savage after the assassination of Heydrich.

Staying back in the relative comfort of the camp had never really been an option when friends and brother officers were prepared to risk their lives doing their duty. Green wondered idly if he would be awarded another Mention in Despatches for getting out of the camp.[4] He didn't really care if it happened or if it didn't.

Eventually a tug on the rope and a whispered command set Green in recumbent motion once again. Soon he came to a widening of the tunnel, where he was instructed to slide off the trolley and onto another one in front of him.

'For goodness sake don't fart. Some of the other men did so at this point and it was most unpleasant. I move on after five more men thank heavens,' whispered a harsh voice with a pronounced Canadian accent.

'Thank heavens I don't feel "windy",' replied Green, rather pleased with this impromptu bit of wit.

'Graveyard humour,' said the Canadian with a chuckle.

'Or whistling in the dark!' replied Green, as he was drawn on to the halfway point of the long tunnel.

Another change of trolley, and Green was off on the last leg of his subterranean journey. His back and neck ached from the effort of remaining rigid on the rails. He came to an abrupt halt and, turning over, looked straight up the shaft, where a faint bluish glow marked freedom.

Soon he was climbing up the wooden ladder towards the sky. At the top of the shaft someone pressed a hand flat on the top of his head.

'Wait a minute. We didn't quite reach the woods. Wait for me to go and hold on to the end of this rope. When I tug it make for the trees in front of you. Don't look back.'

Green waited for a couple of minutes breathing the frosty air. It really was very cold. He froze where he was, as a guard approached, rifle slung over the left shoulder of his greatcoat. His heart began to hammer in his chest as a jackboot thumped the hard snow inches from his hand. Then the muffled figure was gone. Had the lights been on, he would have been easily spotted. The rope jerked his hand and then he was off. He slid out of the shaft into the slush, which quickly chilled his chest. Then he set off at a crouching run over the noisily creaking snow to cover the few yards to the trees, trying not to follow the tracks of the other men through the open snow. He flung himself down under the low branches of a pine and looked around.

At this point the camp lights came back on and the guard towers loomed stark above the wire. He set off into the pine woods before the next man could catch him up. On his right a bulky figure signalled with the rope to the man in the shaft to come ahead.

So this was freedom: a freezing pine forest full of prickly boughs and hollows. He must maintain his direction towards the south-east. His group was detailed not to head for the railway station at Sagan, which lay comparatively close to the camp, but to the next one down the line, a rural halt at Tschiebdorf, where they would regroup. It was considered too obvious and too risky to have a group of twelve disguised prisoners catch a train together from Sagan station.

My God, it was cold. Green kept moving. He emerged from the dense woods in the first grey light of dawn. He knew that he was hours behind schedule. His travel pass was still valid for 25 March and he would head south for Czechoslovakia, which lay about 100 miles away over the mountains.

He moved slowly south, hidden a few yards inside the forest canopy. Other muffled figures joined him from inside the woods until there were twelve men silently walking south through foot-high snowdrifts that quickly soaked and chilled their feet and legs.[5]

A grey light suppressed every feature of the bleak, flat landscape. Belts of trees could be vaguely seen on the other side of the railway line. The chilled men left the cover of the forest as the line curved away into flat land.

The men were close enough to the rails to sense a faint vibration that announced the coming of a train. Without a word they threw themselves flat beside and below the raised ballast. The train wheezed by in a cloud of stream and a blaze of light. Green felt for a second the welcome heat of the engine surging past him and the vibration of dozens of closed vans rattling and banging behind it. At last the train disappeared behind a clump of pines with a shrill whistle and the men stood up and moved forward.

After a march of about 5 miles they came to an ungated crossing and a small platform and waiting room. It was a desolate spot in the middle of a plain. High barred signals showed that no train was due in the immediate future. Powdered snow blew along the platform in little swirls. The men entered the waiting room, where one of them bought twelve tickets to the Czech border. Papers were examined and found to be in order, and the men sat thankfully down on the hard wooden benches that lined the wooden room. Green sat opposite the sulky fire that glowed in the iron grate, occasionally spitting and crackling. It produced almost no heat. The men remembered that they were supposed to be Czech wood mill workers returning from leave and so communicated only in grunts and whispers.

The door to the platform opened and a middle-aged German woman came in. She looked alarmed to see twelve rough-looking men in the room and hastily withdrew onto the platform. Green reckoned that a train was due to arrive soon. Outside the wind had picked up and was beginning to boom in the sky.

All the men heard the clang of the heavy signal arm rising to announce the imminent arrival of a train. The men grumbled a little as they got up and filed out onto the cold platform. A train could be seen coming from the north with a plume of dark smoke rising into the grey sky. It whistled shrilly for the crossing and pulled up with a shriek of brakes at the low platform.

Nobody got off as the men pulled themselves up into a third-class carriage, which was a filthy dull green with many cracked windows. They filled two empty compartments and sat in comparative warmth. The train set off with a jerk and a snort as the wheels slipped momentarily on the icy rails.

As the train moved slowly south it stopped at innumerable small stations. Crowds of noisy schoolchildren climbed aboard and waved cheekily at the shabby men in the compartments. A few grins and waves were enough to satisfy the children's curiosity, and they went on their boisterous way to find empty compartments further down the train.

Tickets were checked and no one took much notice of the drab group of workmen. The countryside was changing from wooded plains to the foothills of what appeared to be a high mountain range. The weak morning sun reflected from high snowfields hundreds of feet above rocky chasms. Green thought that they had covered about 50 miles and knew that they had to get off the train shortly before reaching the major town of Hirschberg. News of the mass escape would obviously have reached towns before villages, and the chance of recapture was greater in Hirschberg than anywhere else.

Green had stayed in a hotel in Hirschberg on business a few years before the war. He even had the hotel receipt somewhere in a drawer at home. He had enjoyed the scenery and the mountain air and remembered the town as a pleasant place with many fine old buildings. He promised himself that he might go there sometime in the future long after this futile war was over. It was such a pity that a civilised country like Germany had been taken over by dangerous fanatics like Hitler and his cronies. Green supposed that he was fighting just as much to restore Germany as to protect his own country.

The train slowed as it curved round a wooded hill. An enamel sign at a crossing indicated that Boberöhrsdorf was 2 kilometres away.[6] Green knew that a dorf was a village and considered it to be a good place to get off the train. The plan would then be to walk over the mountains into Czechoslovakia, avoiding towns and border posts.[7] Inevitably they would have to split up; from now on every man would travel alone, relying on the concentrated rations in his pockets and what he could scrounge in out-of-the-way places.

With flanges squealing and black smoke billowing from its squat chimney, the locomotive came round the bend and applied its brakes to bring the train to a shuddering halt at a small village station. Surrounded by noisy children, the men left the train in small groups, splitting up with no more than a brief glance at each other at the unmanned barrier.

Green set off down a snowy road leading north out of the village. He knew that he had to travel south to the mountains looming on the skyline. First he had to plan how he would get round the village of Boberöhrsdorf in order to climb the lonely mountain pass that led to the Czech border.

About a mile out of the village Green found a deserted half-timbered barn with some mouldy hay inside. He sat on the hay listening to rats scratching in the walls. Outside he could see sunlight reflected from the high mountain meadows that lay between him and Czechoslovakia. Tomorrow he would cross those mountains.

His reveries were broken by a harsh cry, as a bony old cow appeared at the door of the shed. Green slid quietly out of the window and crouched under the wall as the shadow of a farmer slid along the wall over his head. He would have to get through the village in the dusk to lie up on the southern side, in woods if nothing better presented itself.

The sun was a red orb sinking into the mountains as Green walked confidently back into the village. The snow was deeper here than in Sagan because of the increased elevation. It seemed to Green that the remote mountain gods looked down from their rocky crags and pine-covered ridges and mocked him.

A few dim lights were coming on as Green reached Boberöhrsdorf once again. His reconnaissance done, he walked straight along the main street past the drab town hall and police station, past a small park with a few ornamental fir trees, past a few dingy cafés and bars. The snowfields glowed mockingly above him and then began to fade as night drew down. A chill invaded the street with its slushy pavements and desolate dark windows. Green felt shut out in a way he had seldom experienced before.

The thought of a warm hayloft spurred him on. He had rations in his pockets and a good chance of getting away. He must keep his spirits up and bluff his way onwards. Good progress was being made, and soon he would be clear of the village and back in the quiet countryside.

He stumped along the dimly lit street. He saw a turning to the right that would lead him out towards the mountains. Suddenly he saw a bulky human shape in the road in front of him. A tall man in a greatcoat and helmet stood in his way. In his hands was a rifle and he seemed confident. Without any hesitation he asked Green who he was and where he was going. Green replied in his best German, but the soldier pointed his rifle at him and indicated to him to raise his hands above his head. He turned round and marched Green back to the centre of the village to the police station. He was not unfriendly but resolute in doing his duty. Green couldn't blame him at all for what he had done. He couldn't blame himself either; however, Dorothea's words 'silly old fool' came once again to the surface of his mind. At least he knew where he would be spending the night. He hoped that it would be more comfortable than a hayloft.

Hostile looks greeted Green inside the police station. He was bundled into a cell after a quick search, in which his ankles were kicked roughly apart. He was then taken out to a car under armed guard and driven south in the evening darkness to a large nearby town, which turned out to be Hirschberg.

The Hirschberg prison was filthy and unheated. The walls of the old building were damp and flaking. Green saw a number of his fellow escapers there with mixed feelings. He noticed with dismay that the Polish members of the escape party had been forced to stand to attention facing the wall. He was glad that they were safe but sorry that they had been caught. All were cold and hungry, their rations having been taken away from them. They huddled together for warmth on the filthy stone floor of their cell.

At last some thin potato soup in an earthenware crock was brought to them with hunks of stale black bread. The men cheered up immensely when they saw the very pretty Polish girl who brought it. Despite the armed soldiers who accompanied her, she managed to smile and wink at them, as if to say that she was in the same situation as they were. They saw her again from time to time and made a point of always acting with the strictest politeness towards her. This nameless girl was the only bright point of the long, cold, hungry days, which were marked by a faint ray of sunlight that moved across the filthy ceiling from the barred slit of a window high up the wall.

The cold and the isolation were most unpleasant for the handful of men in the cell. From time to time guards took one man away for interrogation, usually returning him the next day. The long hours were punctuated with shrieks in Polish and screams from down the long corridor. When each man returned to the cell, he said that he had not been too badly treated. Each man returned with his pride intact.

When it was Green's turn to be questioned, he was glad to get out of the cell in which he had spent the last four days. He was marched to a light office on an upper floor, where two Gestapo officers questioned him for what seemed hours. They did not strike him but played hot and cold in turns. One would shout at him and threaten him with his riding crop, while the other would pretend to be friendly and make efforts to restrain his colleague.

Towering over Green, the Gestapo officer shouted: 'You English terror flyer! You tried to kill our women and children! You should be truly ashamed of yourself! Where were you going? Who were you going to meet? It would be much better for you and your friends if you were to tell us the truth…'

'I don't know where I am and I don't know in which direction I was going. I demand to be taken back to Stalag Luft III. I am an RAF officer and protected by the Geneva Convention. When the war is over there will be tribunals…'

'Don't threaten us, Sir,' replied the other 'friendly' officer with the silken voice and bad skin. 'You will soon lose the war. We have a new secret weapon that will batter your country into submission in a matter of weeks.'

The interrogation went on in this vein for several tedious hours. Green felt quite detached from the rantings and wheedlings of these two stupidly evil men. He knew that they had the power of life and death over him, but was bored to lethargy by it all. The Gestapo men sensed that they would gain nothing from Green and became bored in their turn. They had used up all their anger in futile threats and still had just enough decency not to hit the stubborn man sitting in front of them.

Green suspected that they knew that the war was lost and were minding their manners for fear of reprisals. They understood fear and were not exempt from it. More weary than angry, they had the guards march Green back to the smelly cell to join his filthy, unshaven mates.

After six days, two of the prisoners were taken out under guard and did not come back. This was the most worrying part of the whole period of imprisonment. The guards' eyes said it all. They refused to meet the prisoners' gaze and shuffled round almost apologetically. Green knew the worst; he suspected that a number of the escapers would be taken out and shot. Something told him that this could be happening all over Germany. He no longer feared for himself; he had tried his hardest and would meet his end with as much dignity as he could summon.

During the eighth night on the cold stone floor huddled in his rags Green had a dream that took him right back to the First World War, to April 1915.[8]

He was lying on the floor of a barn near Ploogsteert in Belgium. He had been told not to move and to clasp a wad of bandages to his lower abdomen. He thought that he must have been in a forward dressing station, because he could hear the moans of the men around him. A thin rain drizzled through gaps in the roof above him. He was reasonably warm in his leather jerkin and not too worried about his wound. A doctor would see him as soon as possible. Blood oozed from behind the bandages and a fiery pain kept him from sleeping, although he felt very tired and thirsty. He wondered what his men were doing without him; in safe hands no doubt. Damned inconvenient being hit by a fragment of rifle grenade; he had heard the report of the rifle just before the searing pain in his abdomen. Perhaps this would be a 'blighty' one, he wondered drowsily. He had never wished for one, but felt so tired. If only he could drift off to sleep…

He woke with a start on the cell floor in Hirschberg Prison. His stomach hurt from lack of food, but was otherwise fine. The irony of his dream struck him. He wouldn't be sent home from here because of a pain in his stomach. He hoped that he would be sent back to the camp at Sagan, but there were absolutely no guarantees.

A grey dawn was struggling through the rusty bars of the cell window. Two sets of boots crashed down the passage and halted outside the cell door. Green's heart leapt as keys were rattled and inserted in the heavy lock and savagely turned.

''Raus, schnell!' barked a harsh voice. Green stood up and stretched with every appearance of casualness despite his beating heart.

'Room service?' he said. The guards looked at him with a hostile glint in their eyes. But they looked directly into his eyes with no shame. 'Good,' thought Green. Today would probably not be his last one.

Green and another officer, Poynter,[9] were marched stiffly along the corridor to the office at the end, where they were given some thin soup and a drink of water as they stood. Then they were taken down some stairs into a courtyard and bundled into a car. Jammed in the back between two guards, they were driven off out of town, with a leather-coated Gestapo man in the front seat beside the driver.

Green knew that there was still a distinct possibility that they would be shot. The guards might have been kept in the dark for all he knew. The car was driven in a northerly direction through belts of woodland and monotonous pine forest. From the occasional shrill train whistle on the right-hand side, Green thought that they were following the railway.

Many opportunities to shoot the prisoners had been passed when the car came to a sudden halt beside the road. There was not a house in sight. The Gestapo man gestured with his Luger for the two prisoners to get out. Flanked by the guards, they did so, and were marched into a grove of birch trees. The Gestapo officer turned and peed into a ditch, then gestured to the prisoners to do so. They turned and did so, feeling hopelessly vulnerable. When they had finished, the Gestapo man roared with laughter and clapped Green on the arm. He looked into his face and spoke one word: 'Sagan'.

Back in the car, Green felt quite weak with relief. He noticed how rank and unwashed the guards smelled and hoped that his odour was even worse. His empty stomach constantly passed gas. By now he couldn't care less if the Germans considered him 'windy' or not.

Sagan came into view round a corner of the forest. The snow had mostly gone, and the grass lay bleached and lifeless in the flat fields. Green could see the huge grain elevator and the railway station with the town behind. The car turned sharply to the left, and Green saw how large the camp had become. Miles of wire fence and dozens of goon boxes marked the perimeter. There was no grass or plants of any kind apart from the endless avenues of pines marching in all directions. The only colourful object was the usual striped guard box at the entrance gate.

Unusually, the senior German officers had come out of the camp and stood tensely in front of the gate. The car drew up in front of them. The prisoners were prodded out of the car and made to sit on the ground with their hands on their heads under the watchful eyes of the guards, as the senior officers and the Gestapo man argued back and forth.

Two things were apparent: von Lindeiner was no longer the camp commandant, and the new commandant, Oberst Braune, definitely did not want two more troublesome escapees back in his camp. After some hysterical shouting and white-faced exchanges, in which 'Hitler's orders' were mentioned time and time again, the Gestapo man impatiently motioned the two bemused prisoners back into the car. The commandant turned on his heel and marched triumphantly away with his entourage of lesser officers.

For a moment Green really thought that his time had come. They were now between the devil and the deep blue sea; nobody wanted them. The Gestapo officer's easiest option would be to have them shot and claim that they had been trying to escape. Their lives hung in the balance.

The car drove off in the direction of the railway station and turned left into the town. So far so good; at least they were not driving out into the country. The drab suburbs of Sagan gave way to the taller and grander buildings of the town centre. The car pulled up outside the police station.

Both men were taken rapidly inside and locked in a cell that was clean and dry. Soup and black bread were brought for them, and they were left in peace. They could hear the Gestapo man's voice raised again in angry argument and a deeper voice with a quieter authority on the telephone. Eventually he slammed down the receiver, and guards came for the prisoners once more. They were put back into the car and driven straight back to the camp.

While they waited for the gates to open, the Gestapo man turned and grinned at Green and his companion. He explained in broken English that the Sagan police chief had defied Hitler's orders in returning the men to the camp. The commandant had given in because it was all becoming too much trouble. They couldn't be kept indefinitely in a civilian prison; there was no money to guard and feed them. They were very fortunate; they would do well to remember that.

Entry into the camp was an anticlimax. There was almost nobody around. No one had seen the dramatic argument at the gate, because the Vorlager lay between the gate and the compound. Both men were immediately sentenced to fourteen days in the cooler for daring to escape. Green regretted von Lindeiner's removal. He too would have put them both into the cooler for the same amount of time, but Green felt that he would have done so more in sorrow than in anger.

The weather had warmed up. The interior of the cooler was reasonably clean and actually not too cold. The blankets thrown in with Green were sufficient to keep out the chill of early spring. Above all, there was no fear. Green was desperately tired and slept long hours in peace. He did not mind being on his own. He had the images of his brief spell of freedom to replay in his mind like precious clips of a wonderful film. He did worry about the fates of some of the other escapers. He had been told nothing and would learn nothing until he was released from the cooler. In the meantime he could recover and dream, sleep and eat the meagre rations that were passed regularly through the grille in his door.

As he lay on the bare boards of his bunk, he pondered on the nature of bravery. He certainly did not consider himself a brave man; he remembered a young private back in the Third Battle of Ypres in 1917.

Captain Green had gone back to the forward dressing station at Pilckem Ridge to check on some of his badly wounded Vickers gunners. He had found them in a terrible state, some mercifully unconscious, others groaning deliriously.

On his way out of the shattered building, his way was blocked by a trouserless man sprawling on the floor with two medics bending over him. One, a doctor with a walrus moustache, was probing into a jagged rent in the man's groin. The prostrate soldier did not make a sound. He was obviously in great pain; his eyes bulged and he bit down hard on a filthy khaki handkerchief.

Eventually the doctor pulled out a jagged bloody piece of shrapnel and dropped it in a bucket with a resounding clang. He quickly stitched the gaping wound together and wrapped a comparatively clean bandage round the man's entire lower stomach. He stood back sweating and spat hard into the bucket.

The man on the floor pushed the medic away and stood shakily up. He pulled up the shredded remains of his trousers and walked to an empty bed, where he lay down. He was a private in the Duke of Cornwall's Light Infantry, a Lewis gunner.

Green bent down to look at him in admiration. Then the man began to talk in a soft West Country accent.

'Bugger me!' he said faintly. 'If I live to be a hundred, I'll never forget that. I could happily have killed that doctor. I suppose it wasn't his fault having no ether.'

'The shell that wounded me killed all my mates, the rest of the gun crew. We used to fire at the Germans' legs before and try not to kill them. If I get back to the front I'll aim at the heart of every German soldier I see…'

Green left the man to sleep. He had a great admiration for him and had no doubt that he would live. Perhaps he would not have the chance to avenge his mates, but he had already done his bit and had strengthened Green's resolve at just the right time, when he was tired and war weary. He owed that man a vote of thanks.

In the autumn of 1918 it was Green's turn to suffer a severe wound. The Germans had overrun virtually all the ground taken by the British in the previous two years. Divisions returning from the Eastern Front reinforced the German drive. Storm troopers rushed speedily over the mangled terrain, bypassing strong points and leaving them to be taken by their comrades. This mad rush forward was desperate and could not be sustained.

The tide of war finally turned well into the last year of the war. Allied divisions beat back the Germans at long last, finding from captured trenches how meagre their supplies were. Many German prisoners were half starved and glad to give themselves up.

Green was by now an acting major and had been awarded the Military Cross in the King's birthday honours.[10] He had survived the tedious repetition of fighting back and forth over the same ground over the previous three and a half years. He was a very experienced officer who could hardly remember what life at home had been like. He was glad to have been decorated and saw the end of the long war in sight.

One autumn day he was strolling across a muddy field a little way behind the lines. He was a touch more relaxed than usual. In a few hundred yards he would be back in the trench to direct his machine gun teams into the forward saps.

'This is a cliché,' he thought. There were a few battered poppies underfoot and a lark singing overhead. The odd German gun was firing, but nothing was coming his way.

Then he heard a whistle that rapidly turned into a roar. A shell landed a few yards away, and Green was plucked off the ground and flung into the air. He landed intact and pulled himself up out of the mud. For some reason he didn't seem to be able to stand and fell breathlessly over into the mud. A searing pain shot through his left heel. He looked down to see blood oozing from a ruined boot. 'Damn,' he thought incoherently pulling off the ruined sole of his left boot.

Blood welded his khaki sock to his violently aching heel. He stood up and hobbled back to the rear dressing station. The shattered heel really hurt. He hoped that the damage was not too serious. He had not hoped for a 'blighty' one and as usual felt that he was letting down the company he commanded. He would be happy to have the wound dressed and go back to the trench and get on with it.

But that was not to be. Green felt overcome by waves of faintness and nausea. The pain was incredible. As he stumbled back, he thought of the man with the wounded groin and tried to pull himself together. It was no good. One of his lieutenants saw him fall and ran out to pick him up and bring him in.

The Medical Officer cut off his boot and cleaned his wound. Green was semi-conscious with shock and pain. He eventually understood that a shell fragment had pierced his left heel and made a horrible mess, but left untouched the main bones and ligaments. He could use his foot when the wound healed, but had to be very careful in the meantime to avoid infection. So he was going home; kicked off the stage before the curtain fell.

In the middle of October 1918 Green was sent home with a gratuity of £120. He was actually relieved to be away from the front, but apprehensive of home life. He had forgotten how to be a civilian; a painful period of adjustment lay ahead of him.

Enough of that reverie; Green would have to relive it all another time. He was in the cooler at Stalag Luft III and soon he would be back among his mates. He hoped that some had managed to get home. He wondered how many had been 'shot while trying to escape'. He had heard other men being thrown into the cells of the cooler during his confinement of nearly two weeks and had identified a few of them as fellow escapers. But that left many more unaccounted for. So Green lay back and even enjoyed his period of monastic solitude. Sometimes he thought back to the comfortable pre-war hotel room in Hirschberg and the contrast with the filthy damp prison.

After two weeks of reflection and rest Green was cast out into the compound. He was assigned a new room, fortunately another two-man room, which he shared with a long-haired theatre director named Kenneth Mackintosh.[11] There was no sign of Dodge or of the majority of the escapers. The sombre mood of the compound hinted of terrible things. Then Green knew. He was taken aside by the Senior British Officer, Group Captain Massey,[12] who sat him down in his room.

'Bernard, there's no easy way to tell you this… Most of our fellow escapers are dead, murdered by the Gestapo, almost certainly on the direct orders of Hitler. Bushell, Long, Catanach… about forty-eight or fifty of them.[13] They were all brave men and were shot down like dogs. We don't know yet who got home; three men are unaccounted for. Twenty-three of you are alive.'

'Day, Dodge, and a number of others have been sent to a concentration camp at Sachsenhausen[14] in clear violation of the Geneva Convention. The rest are here, mainly still in the cooler.'

'The Nazis are not going to get away with this. When this war ends we who survive will bear witness to the murder of our comrades and must help to bring their killers to justice.'

'Von Lindeiner has been relieved of his command. He was beside himself after the escape and has suffered some sort of breakdown. The Nazis are accusing him and the senior camp officers of profiteering, of smuggling fine wines and champagne into the camp for their own use.'

'The new commandant, Braune, told me that forty-eight escapers had been "shot while trying to escape". He could not tell me how many had been wounded and could not look me in the eye. A list will be going up soon and we have permission to build a monument to the murdered escapers. I can't go on…'

Massey looked out of the window at the wire. He was struggling not to break down. Green felt the same. He wondered why younger, fitter and more able men had been chosen to die, when old duffers like him would live on. They would not break his spirit; the Nazis were desperate and could not hold out much longer on two fronts. Soon the Allies would land somewhere in France and beat the Hun back to the Fatherland. They would join up with armies fighting in Italy and chase the Nazis back to the smouldering ruins of Berlin. One day the prisoners would be free and their captors held accountable for their crimes. He had to believe this in order to keep going.

In the meantime the compound was a drab and dismal place. As soon as he could, Green wrote a letter home to reassure his family that he was safe; he also wrote one to Evelyn. He could not refer in any way to the escape, but he emphasised, as usual, that he was fit and well. He hinted at the tragic events of the past few weeks in an oblique way: 'I have certainly been more fortunate than the commandant of our special police though it has come to much the same in the end – do you remember his talk in the cinema at Marlow?'

He spent much of the letter describing Mackintosh and the theatre posters that now hung on the walls of his room. In his future letters he would have much to say about the camp theatre productions, which he saw but took no major part in. There wasn't much more to write about.

He wondered where Adrian was. He congratulated him on his speedy promotion to captain in the Reconnaissance Corps[15] and knew that the invasion of France would soon be on the cards.

Life would never return to normal in the compound; too many of the old faces were gone. News continued to arrive from newly captured airmen: Berlin was being reduced to rubble, the Americans were doing a great job bombing German industry, strange new flying bombs were raining down on London.[16] The Russians were continuing their westwards advance, and the Allies were fighting their way up the spine of Italy.

With all this positive news, the fate of the prisoners hung in the balance. Would the Nazis hold the airmen as a bargaining card or would they let them be taken over by the Red Army? Would there be mass executions as supplies ran low and the increasingly desperate Nazi hierarchy decided to wipe the slate clean in their fanaticism?

Green refused to worry. All escape attempts were shelved on the orders of the Senior British Officer. The time of gentlemen adventurers winning the grudging admiration of their gaolers for their daring escape attempts was well and truly over. The new commandant was fair but could never be relied on to shield his prisoners from higher authority. Not even von Lindeiner had been able to do that. Broili and Simoleit[17] were increasingly withdrawn and evasive, worried about their own futures as well as those of their charges.

In the meantime the show went on. Mackintosh produced *I Killed the Count* and *Blithe Spirit*. Green considered the standard to be amazingly high and profited from his friendship with Mackintosh to obtain tickets to nearly all the performances.

On a more sombre note, the commandant allowed the officers to build a monument to the fifty officers shot by the Gestapo after the escape. The names and ranks of all fifty men were carefully inscribed in black letters on the face of the monument.

Small bronze urns containing the individual sets of ashes began to arrive at the camp. Each was marked with the officer's name, date of death and the name of a town. With typical unconscious Teutonic thoroughness, the murderers had ensured that their crimes could be traced after the end of the war. Green learned that Bushell and his French escape partner, Scheidhauer,[18] had almost reached the French border. Their urns were marked 'Saarbrucken'; others came from as close as Breslau. These urns were looked after by Group Captain Massey and later by his successor after his repatriation on medical grounds.

The reluctant Silesian spring turned into a hot Silesian summer. Slush became dust, but the flanking army of pines that stretched away for mile after dreary mile did not change at all. The camp was hemmed in as ever, the only difference being the beautiful azure sky from which the hot sun beamed for day after monotonous day.

Two tunnels were started, codenamed George and Margaret. Green was keen to help with the distribution of the excavated sand but was ordered not to take part. Having participated in the earlier escape, he was a marked man. He contented himself with his study of Russian and with attending rehearsals and theatrical productions produced by his old friend John Casson,[19] son of Dame Sybil Thorndike.

Summer dimmed to a chilly autumn. Green cursed the implacable pines that surrounded the camp. They revealed nothing, gave out nothing. He hoped never to see another pine tree in his life. In moments of quiet frustration he visualised himself swinging a huge axe and splitting endless pine logs.

Mare's tales high in the sky warned of the coming of the biting east wind. Flurries of lazy snow covered the dull ground before being trodden to slush by hundreds of badly shod feet walking round the inside of the wire. Many men now wore rough clogs with no socks. Green kept his best shoes in readiness for the eventual evacuation of the camp.

7. The Black March

Have been having 25° to 30 degrees of frost here.
All the very best - here's to our meeting next year. BG

Christmas was celebrated with a weary familiarity by nearly all the officers in the camp. While many felt that it would be their last winter in captivity, others were resigned to wait for something to happen. Green had worked out that the Russians could not be very far off. He felt that they had exactly the same designs on Poland as the Nazis. Remembering the former treaty between Germany and Russia at the beginning of the war, which would have divided the country in half, he knew that the Russians would now take the whole of Poland under their iron rule.

The prisoners would be a useful bargaining tool for the Nazis. At worst they could be used for a shield against Allied bombing. At best they could be traded for a certain amount of leniency at the end of the war. One other possibility existed: they could be shot down like rats by a desperate and crazed Nazi hierarchy in mad revenge for the loss of the 'Thousand Year Reich'. Speculation was a waste of time. Chance would be a leading factor in the fates of thousands of Allied prisoners.

January dragged its frigid feet. At the end of the month Green knew that something was up. In his letters and postcards he maintained the status quo. Yes, he was fit and well. He was enjoying his theatrical experiences and hoped that the war would soon be over. His world had contracted to a weary, cold existence, with miles walked every day round the wire and kit kept clean and serviceable. He continued to keep his best shoes and socks in reserve for whatever was going to happen.

Senior officers were briefed at the end of January and extra rations issued. Kit was to be packed and all officers were to parade in a state of readiness to move out at dawn on 27 January 1945.

Rank upon rank of emaciated men stood on the frozen ground with their breath pluming into a grey sky. There was no excitement, merely resignation that life could get a lot worse very soon. Most held bundles of clothes and food. All wore a strange variety of hats, caps and even scraps of cloth knotted at the corners. All kinds of tattered greatcoats and tunics were on parade. A few men had almost immaculate uniforms with the wings or brevets visible. Some men wore full beards and some were clean shaven; most wore a filthy stubble above the ragged scarves and mufflers with which they were trying hard to keep warm. All around them the cold seeped in. Yet not one man stamped his feet on the frozen earth. They all waited to go, thankful for a change of any sort. Few dreaded leaving the camp.

At last the German guards marched reluctantly up to the assembled officers. Their uncertainty was palpable. Many of the old soldiers were reminded of the Eastern Front and the Russian winter. Here they were about to embark on a long march with hundreds of enemy prisoners who would not hesitate to take advantage of them in any way they could, from killing them to distracting and humiliating them. They knew that the game was nearly over.

Green was interested to see that Feldwebel Glemnitz[1] was attached to the officers from the North Compound. The gates were finally pulled open and the march began. For the first time in years Green marched up to the main gate through the Vorlager parallel to the subterranean route taken by Harry all those months ago. He barely glanced over at the cooler, now standing empty for the first time since the compound had opened. Glad of his carefully preserved shoes, he marched out of the main gate, past the striped and unoccupied sentry boxes on each side. A wall of dense pine trees stretched away on either side of the rough track, which soon turned to the south.

It was obvious that the ragged column was not heading for the railway station. Green heard the name 'Spremberg' passed between the guards and knew that they were in for a long cold march. Soon some of the men began to slow down and straggle. Crude sledges with kit and rations were abandoned in snowdrifts beside the rutted and frozen road. After a couple of hours men started to fall behind and sit down on the hard surface of the road with utter exhaustion etched on their faces. Green heard shots from the back of the column.

Glemnitz grimaced as the echoes rebounded from the forest edge. He stalked to the rear of the long column with a face like thunder and raged at one or two of the guards. As the march continued a man would occasionally collapse beside the road to be left lying where he fell. With the best will in the world, no man had the energy to help him. After a few hours the occasional guard would collapse with a clatter onto the frozen road. He too would be left to his fate. Survival was too precious to waste on no hopers.

Only Glemnitz had the determination to keep going up and down the column exhorting both guards and prisoners to keep going. Green noticed some of the younger officers helping the older guards along, carrying their kit and even their rifles for them. He realised that the effects of malnutrition were not confined to the prisoners.

As he swung silently along, his left heel began to throb. Pain flared from time to time and he thought ironically how his wounded heel had saved him back in 1918. Now it was becoming a liability. He was determined not to go down on the road and die of exposure. Pain made him realise that he was alive; it kept him awake and warned him of the consequences of falling out.

Green realised that he missed von Lindeiner. He would have liked at least to have said goodbye to him. He wondered what would become of this decent and elderly man who was rumoured to have refused to join the Nazi Party. He thought that he had a lot in common with this man, whom he had been forced to think of as his enemy. Meanwhile, there was Glemnitz; the Feldwebel was an example of encouragement and support. Green supposed that he should have hated him. He remembered reading how the Good Soldier Schweik always made a point of saluting the officer's uniform hanging on the back of the door instead of the man. Green thought that he should hate the uniform and all it stood for rather than the man inside it.

Dusk fell as the column straggled painfully into a village. The exhausted officers squatted on the cold cobbles while Glemnitz vanished into a derelict factory, which loomed in the darkness a hundred yards away. The men were hungry and extraordinarily tired. They did not relish the thought of a night under a thin blanket on frozen cobbles. Raised voices came from inside the factory, and Glemnitz strode out beckoning to the men to come in. He pointed to the filthy straw on the floor of the stables and ordered the reluctant guards to distribute rations to the prisoners. Small fires were lit and men messed in small groups, sharing stale black bread, acorn coffee and the carefully hoarded remains of Red Cross food parcels. Glemnitz pointed to what had once been the factory's offices and shouted 'Abort'. Men clapped appreciatively, and a few walked into the match-boarded rooms, where they dropped their trousers in the dark. A few men threw old newspapers into the offices and muffled shouts of 'Thank you' rose from the shadows.

Most men lay down to sleep where they were. Green made sure that he was away from the doors and glassless windows before collecting some straw to protect himself from the cold striking upwards from the cement floor. As he fell asleep, he heard the usual rats running through the straw and thought back to the trenches. 'What was an old codger like him doing on a forced march in the depths of a central European winter?' he wondered. He felt no self-pity as he drifted into oblivion.

The wind soughed around the derelict building, seeking exposed flesh and human weakness. In the cold grey dawn the officers got stiffly to their feet, feeling chilled and light-headed. But three did not rise. They had died of exposure and fatigue during the night and were left lying just inside the broken factory door when the column formed up after a meagre breakfast for another bleak day's forced march.

The searing cold abated slightly as fat snowflakes swirled down from a glaucous sky. Wet snow clung to every surface of the marching men. From time to time someone would bend over and vomit onto the road. Dysentery was beginning to spread among the weakened men. As the long day wore on, some of the sicker men were picked up and dumped in a decrepit cart that had been commandeered from somewhere. Men continued to fall out and disappear into the forests beside the road. By now the guards were too preoccupied with their own survival to bother about anything else. There were no more shots, just low mutterings from time to time.

The blizzard continued all day. Everyone was cold, damp and miserable. Men fell asleep on their feet when the column stopped and had to be roused by their friends. Green realised by the somewhat exotic bad language that he heard from time to time that there were Americans in the column. He quietly tried out some of the words for himself as he hobbled grimly along: 'When will this goddamn snow ease off? What's that son of a bitch Hitler up to?' It amused him to repeat these mindless phrases in his own world isolated by swirling snow and icy wind.

At last the long day seemed to die of exhaustion. The bone-weary column straggled into a town. Glemnitz found everybody a billet and Green lay down beneath the wooden counter of a shop. He was drifting off to sleep when he heard shouts and angry expletives all round him. An SS private prodded him onto his feet and kicked him out into the street. He lay down in the gutter wrapped in his thin blankets and fell asleep almost immediately, to wake hours later chilled to the bone and ravenously hungry. Sleeping men lay all over the street, their humped bodies reminding him of the First World War dead.

Guards picked their way through the prone bodies dropping rations on the cobbles. Green saw that most of the snow had melted and that his blankets were soaked with slush. He sat up and shared a parcel with two bleary pilots.

As hundreds of weary men stood up painfully, Green heard almost every filthy word that he had ever known in his life. Part of him was detached enough to be amused by the antics of his fellow sufferers. He was as stiff and as cold as the next man; he suspected that he was coming down with 'flu. He would just have to carry on as long as he could. The alternative would be to lie up in the dark forest with nothing to eat and only snow to drink.

It was at the grim beginning of the third day of the march that Green saw a remarkable sight. One of the guards, an older man with a haggard face, was obviously ill. He shook uncontrollably and could hardly stand. A young British officer took his rifle and leather webbing and carried them until the man felt better. He then handed the rifle back to the guard, who took it carefully and politely only to fling it into a ditch full of muddy water. The German then bowed respectfully to the British officer and walked off to the rear of the column. Green never saw him again.

The sun shone weakly on a sodden landscape. There was a little warmth in the air, and many of the marchers revived somewhat. Green's wet shoes cracked on his feet but no longer felt like stiff boxes. He estimated that they were moving west and were not heading for Bavaria. His clothes were filthy and he itched. From time to time his temperature rose and he felt hot all over one minute and cold the next. He could not feel sorry for himself; but he would have loved a wash, a shave and a warm bed for the night.

On the fourth day of the march the Americans parted company with the straggling mass of men. They appeared to be heading south, while the British and their Allies continued in a north-westerly direction. Priebus and Muskau had been passed as in a bad dream, and the snow began to fall once again, muffling the monotonous tramp of worn shoes on the hard road. Many of the men regretted the sledges they had left behind after the brief thaw.

Green was getting used to the fact that his world had shrunk to a few feet around him. For hours he could see only the shrouded shapes of the two men shuffling on each side of him. At times he found it difficult to remember who they were. He hadn't seen Group Captain Wray, the Senior British Officer, for three days. At least he was not suffering from frostbite. He had always had an exceptionally good circulation, had swum in the Thames in winter and had even rather enjoyed it.

On what Green estimated was 1 February the column arrived at Spremberg after the agonising five-day forced march. At last the weary men were taken into a barracks, filthy and vandalised as it was, and given hot soup. It took hours for them to thaw out and relax. What mattered was the here and now; they were out of the frost and the snow and could wrap themselves in comparatively dry blankets to ward off the pervasive cold.

Next day after Appel the men formed fours and left under a depleted guard for the railway station. They were taken into a snowy siding and ordered to climb up into wooden covered vans with arched roofs. Red Cross parcels were thrown in seemingly at random but no water. Green wondered how long they would be incarcerated in the train and where they were going.

When all the sliding doors had been slammed shut and padlocked, the locomotive panting at the head of the train gave a thin shriek and jerked the long train into motion. Inside the vans the men took turns to sit and to lie down. A smelly fug pervaded the atmosphere and it became tolerably warm. One corner of each van was chosen as a latrine and it was put to constant use by the men with dysentery.

'Constipated or squeamish?' asked a thin airman with an enormous handlebar moustache.

'Concrete factory,' replied Green. 'Thank heaven I've avoided dysentery so far.'

He was reasonably comfortable as the train shook and rattled its slow way across central Germany. The wheel flanges squealed and one wheel banged incessantly. The only occasional sign of life from outside the train was the tinny ding of the level-crossing warning bells, which changed note as the train roared over small rural roads.

After a few hours thirst became the problem. No one had any water at all. The few drips from melting snow that found their way into the van were soon licked off the walls and floor. Those men near the metal ventilators fared a little better than the rest because of the condensation.

Green managed to sleep through almost all the first night on the train. Much of the second day was spent in a siding waiting for something to happen. The van doors remained locked and the remaining rations were carefully shared out.

Eventually the train set off and crawled through what seemed to be miles of marshalling yards and industrial sidings. Green could see the devastation through the crack between the planks in the van's side. Surely the war could not last much longer.

On the third long day the train came to a halt in Hanover. The prisoners were so thirsty that they could hardly talk and so waited for the doors to slide open for hour after long hour. At last water was delivered and handed round so that everyone who was conscious managed to drink at last. Green had never appreciated water so much in his life.

The men were reassured that their journey was nearly over. The words 'Marlag und Milag' were endlessly repeated. One of the Fleet Air Arm officers remembered that it was a camp for naval prisoners somewhere north of Bremen. This gave some hope to the cramped and smelly men who were sick of railways, Germany and each other.

Next day many of the men had to be helped out of the railway van onto the ground by their mates and by the guards. Green felt stiff and achy but relieved that most of his 'flu had passed. He saw a number of sick officers carried across the snowy sidings on stretchers and had no idea who they were or if they were dead or alive. He stretched his tired limbs and prepared to move.

Hours later the snow had turned to a persistent drizzle. Hundreds of men waited in the darkness outside the barbed-wire gate of yet another prison camp. They stamped their feet and turned up their sodden collars. 'Hurry up and wait,' thought Green as he gnawed on some stale black bread. The men were not talking to each other; each was an island of desperation and boredom. Surely something would have to happen soon.

After six long hours the gates shuddered open and the men shuffled in. The huts smelled of disinfectant and had been swept. Each mess was issued with tins of Klim and some scraps of wood and coal were found.

The Senior British Officer, Group Captain Larry Wray,[2] called on each mess in turn to tell them: 'Welcome to Tarmstedt. We are a few miles north of Bremen in Marlag und Milag Nord.[3] I apologise for the wait. The camp was filthy and infested with vermin and I insisted that it was made fit for us. It wasn't easy and I had no way of telling you. We shall be here for some time. The war cannot last long. We must do nothing to provoke our hosts at this point.'

The thin mustachioed pilot spoke up: 'They must watch their step with us too. When we are liberated we shall remember who our friends are and who helped us.'

Life settled down in the sparse barracks. The Germans made every attempt to run the camp efficiently, with regular Appels and inspections, but it was becoming obvious that their morale was low and that they were only going through the motions. Many of the guards who had been on the march had gone, to be replaced by young boys and old men. It was not worth making attempts to escape; conditions outside the camp were possibly even more desperate and unsafe than they were under the disciplined eye of Group Captain Wray, who seemed to be taking more and more responsibility for the running of the camp. Green saw the role of the prisoners as that of pawns in an enormous and chaotic chess game. The Germans were becoming close to being checkmated and were running out of options. Perhaps one more desperate move would see the end of it.

That move came about four weeks after the prisoners had arrived at Tarmstedt. At short notice they were told to form up on the parade ground and given an hour to collect their kit and rations. Many of the men had recovered their health and some of their strength. The weather was turning warmer with the signs of early spring. Green realised that it would soon be a year since the escape from Stalag Luft III. His shoes had somehow held together, and he still had his tattered Polish greatcoat. His 'flu had gone and he had even gained a little weight in the camp. There had been no chance to write letters home since January. He wondered if his son, Adrian, was in Germany by now.

A rumour that they were off to the seaside circulated round the camp. Green took stock of his kit and of himself. He was 58 years old, stocky, and underweight. His skin was filthy and he was lousy. His shoes were just about holding together. He had a ragged greatcoat that hung from his shoulders like a shroud, his very worn RAF tunic, a khaki sweater with many holes, a pair of battledress trousers, which had been taken up almost to the knee, two reasonable pairs of socks, a filthy shirt and a vest that he wouldn't clean his car with in peacetime.

He was reasonably fit, yet he had a persistent cough. Although his face sagged in places, he still looked like a man in his forties. He felt reasonably optimistic that he could make this march and survive the war, if nothing bad intervened.

He looked forward to going home, but he wondered how Dorothea was after nearly five years. Would she still be so critical? Would she actually want him to come home from the wars? Only time would tell.

The march took the men north towards Lübeck away from the area of Bremen. Allied aircraft flew regularly over the column as it snaked north. One day an RAF Typhoon swooped low over the men, who trudged on without their guards, who had dived into the ditches on each side of the road.

Many of the prisoners flung themselves onto the road as the crackle of machine guns erupted from the leading edge of the plane's wings. For a second there was silence before the fighter rose high in the air and flew away to the west. Shakily men struggled to pick themselves up from the dusty road. A blackbird sang its liquid notes from a nearby apple tree. Two men had been slightly wounded in the raid and were given first aid by the medic. Four men lay sprawled in the road in an untidy pile. They had all been killed instantly by the .303 bullets; blood leaked from numerous wounds. All were naval officers who had been marching at the rear of the column talking in low voices before the plane suddenly swooped down, randomly to take their lives. Green registered the intense look of surprise on one of the men's face.

With a depleted number of guards, the column struggled on. One more night in a filthy, draughty billet; one more issue of Red Cross parcels and Klim; one more journey across a depressing and depressed landscape. At last they arrived at the camp outside Lübeck; broken windows, rats, lack of sanitation and broken furniture once again.

Green felt the proximity of the sea. He could not see or hear it but could faintly smell it. The quality of the light to the north indicated that the land finally stopped there. Spring had arrived at last, and he felt that some sort of resolution was near. The camp was adequate after much sweeping and scrubbing and browbeating of the guards to provide planks to repair shattered windows and broken doors. The leaves broke on the trees and the camp no longer woke up every morning to frost.

The Senior British Officers were taking increasing command of the camp. All the German officers from Stalag Luft III had been recalled to more active service elsewhere, and their replacements seemed awed by their captives. They knew that it would soon all be over and very much hoped that they would not be ordered to shoot any of their charges. They grew increasingly tense and walked around the camp with their eyes cast down.

'Cheer up, old chap; it may never happen,' said Green to one of them. He was rewarded by a look of utter blankness and incomprehension.

April turned into May. The days were growing longer and warmer and the prisoners, despite their regular washing and dhobying, grew crustier and smellier. Lice, fleas and ticks became the new enemy. Rations were just about adequate, but no one was gaining weight. It would have been easy to sit back in exhaustion and wait for the war to end. Green continued to take regular exercise; several circuits of the rusty wire were the norm as well as press-ups and the usual callisthenics.

The morning of 2 May 1945 dawned like almost every day in nearly five years of captivity. The only difference was the noisy presence of many low-flying Luftwaffe fighters, 109s and Focke-Wulfs, which buzzed over the camp heading south-east. Crowds of civilians coming from the direction of Lübeck shambled along the road past the camp. They were shabbily dressed and carried and pushed their meagre belongings. A man abandoned a rusty pram outside the camp gate then straggled hopelessly on after the others.

Gunfire could be heard nearby, and at around 5 p.m. a swarm of Allied aircraft flew low overhead. A lone Spitfire came in behind the others and waggled its wings over the camp as if to reassure the ragged men that help was at hand.

At a quarter past five on a glorious luminous spring evening a column of dark green armoured cars unhurriedly approached the camp gates.[4] A tall officer could be seen in the turret of the leading vehicle directing operations. Armoured cars peeled deliberately left and right from the column and took up positions facing the wire with their stubby guns elevated.

The leading car drove straight through the flimsy camp gate, scattering wire and wood in all directions. The few German guards threw down their weapons and shot their hands into the air. They were totally ignored by the liberating soldiers and the cheering prisoners.

Green found himself strangely shy and tongue-tied. He looked in awe at these young soldiers, clean shaven in immaculate uniforms. They all had their dark blue Armoured Corps berets on at the same angle.

'You are free, courtesy of the 11th Armoured Division, British Army. Stay in the camp and we will sort you out as soon as we can. God save the King!'

Group Captain Wray stepped forward and saluted the officer in the turret. The officer, a major, climbed down, and the two men solemnly shook hands. A ragged cheer rose from the even more ragged airmen, naval officers and the few Army officers in the camp.

The German guards and their officers were locked in their barracks by the liberating soldiers. Wray presented the major with a complete list of those officers present in the camp, and rations were issued as quickly as possible. The men swarmed back to their messes and, after a hasty but sumptuous meal, prepared themselves for evening parade.

Hundreds of relieved officers stood in ranks of four on the now floodlit Appel ground. Outside the camp the occasional explosion and burst of small-arms fire indicated that all was not yet quite settled. Green smelled burning and reckoned that a few scores were still being resolved. He had no wish to retaliate. When asked by a captain to tell him who the bad guards were, he replied that he was not aware of any in this camp; by and large he told the truth. The people he wanted to see punished were the SS and Gestapo men who had ruthlessly shot down the fifty defenceless escapees just over a year before.

The parade came to attention as smartly as it could. The Major spoke in a loud firm voice.

'As you probably all know by now, Hitler is dead. He took his own life in Berlin a week ago. The Thousand Year Reich is at an end. We must still be careful. There are pockets of resistance and some of the Nazis still have scores to settle. You have all played your part in this victory, a magnificent part.'

'Be assured that we will seek justice. We shall find the killers of your comrades and prosecute them under the law. They shall not escape the consequences of their cowardly acts. We shall be asking you to tell us what you know when you are back in England. It will be painstaking and it will be tedious but, without your help, these murderers will walk free.'

'Stay in this camp under the command of Group Captain Wray. We shall arrange for you all to be flown home to England, to hot baths and to your families. You must continue to be patient having come so far. You will be shortly issued with new uniforms and kitbags. Tonight you will sleep as free men.'

Green felt exhausted beyond words as he lay on his bunk in the hut with four other officers snoring and whistling their way to oblivion. He felt happy, but there was also the tremendous feeling of anticlimax and uncertainty about what lay ahead.

Three days later Green felt like a new man. He had had what the barber had laughingly called a haircut and had been deloused. His new uniform fitted him quite well and would do for now. The rest of his new kit was in two new white kitbags and ready to go.[5] The days in camp had dragged.

All Germans had been taken away, and Green ventured out of the camp for a short walk on the plain that surrounded the camp. The few trees were in full leaf and the birds were singing. In the blue sky the contrails of American bombers scratched the heavens. It was quiet now; the trickle of refugees had ceased, and there were British soldiers everywhere. Green still felt isolated by his experiences. He would find it hard to carry on a normal conversation for a long time in the future.

There were goodbyes to say and addresses to exchange. Then lorries drove up to the camp and officers and their kit were loaded aboard for their flight home to England. In the roaring, vibrating DC3 Green felt strangely at home. Surely, in another lifetime years ago, hadn't he flown against the Nazis before becoming earthbound? He had fallen from the sky to pass under the earth in order to be free.

8. 'There's No Discharge in the War!'

In a cloud of rubber smoke the DC3 landed at Northolt. Green still felt isolated and entirely out of context. In a way he dreaded his homecoming.

The officers were driven to a hut on the edge of the airfield, where they were given a cup of tea and a biscuit and a warm but understated welcome by a grey-haired senior RAF officer. He explained that the debriefing was extremely important and that all the information the ex-prisoners could give was vital to the investigation of the murders of their comrades.

Green's interview lasted several days and left him far more drained than any of his encounters with the Gestapo. He was questioned kindly and firmly but the memories were too fresh in his mind to let him relax. He was glad when he was released with a rail travel warrant for Bourne End.

On a brilliantly sunny May day he sat on a worn carriage seat on the Marlow Donkey. He had changed from the Plymouth train at Maidenhead, and the two-coach branch-line train had rattled along the branch through Furze Platt and Cookham. Green wondered idly if the painter Stanley Spencer was still wheeling his old black pram with his easel and arguing acrimoniously with the toll keeper on the bridge. The quality of the light changed as the train boomed over the girder bridge that spanned the Thames. The sun glinted on the river as it swept its curving course between Berkshire and Buckinghamshire. Green sensed the wooded Chiltern Hills that rose behind the village of Bourne End. He could smell the quiet river and the trees that drooped on its banks. With a clatter of points and a squeal of brakes, the train pulled up at the platform of Bourne End station.

As Green opened the heavy door he could hear the familiar announcement: 'Bourne End, change for Marlow.'

He left his two kitbags at the station to be delivered later on. He was appalled at the unkempt appearance of the station, unpainted and shabby. He remembered the poster that stated 'Bovril for old buffers', which had graced the down side of the station for several years. He had composed the slogan and was surprised when it won the competition and was chosen for his home station.

Green walked through the booking hall, past the bicycle rack and out of the station. He turned left at the Station Hotel, calling out 'Hello Len!' to the rather astonished landlord. A couple of hundred yards towards the village centre he passed Lloyd's Bank on the right and swung into Wharf

Lane at the allotments. In front of him he saw Cortegar, the house that had been given to him and Dorothea as a wedding present in 1916.

The peeling wooden wicket gate made the familiar creaking sound as he pushed it open, but no one rushed out to greet him. Dorothea was in the kitchen. Of course she was pleased to see him, but there was no real warmth in her greeting. Green thought that she looked thin and much older. In the five years that he had been away she had become an old woman with little of the sparkle of her younger years.

She did not quite know how to treat her husband. They had grown apart from each other, and Green realised that absence had not made the heart grow fonder. He became even more withdrawn than he had been, almost afraid to speak in case he upset the delicate balance of their distant relationship.

After a few weeks Green thought that he must escape again. Dorothea was as kind as she could be but incapable of turning back the years. Besides, he had no job to go to at Soho Mill. His brother-in-law Sedgwick had died, leaving Green's sister Lorna penniless. The mill had been run down after the war, and its labour force was contracting in the new austerity. Green decided that he had to go elsewhere to earn a living. He would always provide for his wife but could no longer sit at home.

The climax came some time after Green's return. A letter came inviting him to Buckingham Palace to attend the Garden Party. Uniforms were to be worn, and Green's new medal ribbons arrived soon afterwards in the post. He asked Dorothea if she would mind sewing them onto his tunic for him, because he knew that she would make a much better job of it than he would.

All Dorothea's frustrations boiled over, all the worry of the previous five years and the anticlimax of her husband's homecoming. Yes, she would mind very much sewing on his wretched ribbons. Hadn't he had enough of them in the first war? Why didn't he go out and get himself a job? She had forgotten that Green was still a Flight Lieutenant in the Royal Air Force and was being paid as such until he was demobbed.

So Green set out to earn a living. His son, Adrian, was coming home, having been recently demobbed from his rank of Captain in the Reconnaissance Corps. His daughter Catherine's husband Clive, a Captain in the Hampshires, was due back from India any day. Dorothea would not be left alone, and Green would continue to provide for her. Reluctantly he knew that both would be happier if they lived separate lives.

Green decided to start a taxi business, with a grant from an ex-service men's association, in Chichester, where Evelyn now lived. He would ferry airmen around from a nearby airfield and live frugally, visiting his son and daughter and his wife when she wanted to see him. He had to admit that he had escaped for the last time.

Green soon settled into his new life in Chichester. He rented a couple of rooms from the Haberer family and drove his taxi around the countryside of West Sussex. He felt a new kind of freedom and a lightness of heart that he had seldom experienced before. Many of his clients were RAF personnel, and life was quiet, interesting and fairly undemanding.

He had left the RAF somewhat reluctantly, but he kept his uniform immaculate in a cupboard. His service life was over at last, and he began to make quite a good living in post-war austerity Britain. He was concerned that his wife, Dorothea, was now quite seriously ill. She did not really want to have much to do with him any more and naturally that saddened him. His son, Adrian, was married in 1948, and he and his new wife, Alison, moved into Cortegar, where they looked after Dorothea and were company for her. Green knew that it was not easy; Dorothea was becoming very ill and sometimes quite hard to live with. Bernard and Dorothea Green were photographed together for the last time at their son Adrian's wedding in Little Marlow church.

In 1951 Dorothea died of cancer. Green was sad and relieved at the same time. He had been powerless to take any other course of action and was sorry that her life had ended this way.

After a decent interval he proposed marriage to Evelyn Haberer, the daughter of his landlord. She was intelligent, attractive and artistic, and she clearly loved him. They were married in Chichester and, just over a year later, their daughter Jennifer was born. They had bought a house in Westhampnett Road with a large garden and lived very happily.

Green kept in touch with his son, Adrian, and his daughter, Catherine. He was prospering in a modest sort of way and, as he approached pensionable age, decided to retire. He took Evelyn and Jennifer on a holiday down to South Devon, where Adrian had moved with his family after being promoted to the position of sales manager of Tuckenhay Paper Mill, one of the last mills to produce hand-made paper. Green was proud that his son had continued in the paper trade. There had been Greens connected with paper-making in Kent right back to the sixteenth century.

The senior Greens also visited a cousin in Hampshire and Catherine and her husband and family who lived near Southampton. The 1950s soon became the 1960s, as Britain began to emerge from its post-war gloom.

Green was saddened to hear of the death of Johnnie Dodge in 1960. His friend had continued in politics but had never succeeded in becoming a Member of Parliament. Green hadn't seen a lot of him since the end of the war but would miss him.

In 1963 half-submerged memories of the tragic events after the escape from Stalag Luft III were brought to the fore by the release of the film *The Great Escape*. Green happily accepted the invitation to attend the premiere of the film at the Odeon Cinema in the West End of London on Tuesday, 20 June 1963. He enjoyed it, saying only that, although the escape took place in the winter, the film portrayed it happening in brilliant summer sunshine. He said that the film reproduced the atmosphere of the camp very well; he was not overly concerned with the details. He did not mention that the actor Donald Pleasence, who played the part of the forger with failing eyesight, bore an uncanny physical resemblance to himself. Like Green, Pleasence had himself been a prisoner of war.

As the 1960s wore on, England won the World Cup, London became the swinging capital of Europe, and Green's formerly robust health began to decline. He was well into his seventies when he was diagnosed with Parkinson's disease. He found it hard to move around and became very bent. His mind started to crumble; the effects of ten years of the most acute deprivation, stress and danger produced an extreme form of depression known as melancholia. As Kipling had so rightly said in his poem 'Boots': 'There's no discharge in the war!'

To the end of his life Green was faithfully cared for by his loving wife Evelyn and his daughter Jennifer. His sense of humour never left him. In the mid-1960s the family moved to a fine modern house in the Somerdale area on the northern edge of Chichester. Green joked that you couldn't always trust the eggs at the local shop because 'some are stale and some are not...' Bernard Green, MC, BA (Cantab.), died on 2 November 1971 and was cremated on 5 November. It would have greatly appealed to his sense of humour to realise that he had died on All Souls' Day and that he was cremated on Guy Fawkes Night.

Appendix 1: Now It Can Be Told

Bernard Green, MC

After the war Bernard wrote a very short piece describing his escape.

After getting out of the tunnel – you will have read that it came out in the open instead of into the wood – it was horribly open and the man at the end of the rope pulled it for warning. I lay flat, and a guard walked by quite near. I do not know how he did not hear my breath coming in pants – I did! After he had gone, I crawled into the wood. The frozen snow seemed to make enough noise to raise the dead.

About twelve of us collected in the wood and walked about five miles through the woods to a station south of Sagan: very heavy going; snow halfway up to our knees at times. At one time we lay flat by a railway track while a train passed in what seemed a blaze of light.

We were in the Waiting Room at the station (by the way, we were Czech workmen in all sorts of costumes) when a German woman came in and then withdrew very hurriedly – I suppose we looked a bit too tough! We had a strange journey of about fifty miles by train along with children going to school etc. No one took much notice of us. We got out at a station just short of Hirschberg (I had stayed there between the wars and still have the hotel bill!).

I lay up for several hours trying to find a way round the next village but it was hopeless. The snow was waist high in the fields. Eventually, I decided to walk straight through and got to the last turning when a German soldier stopped me and, after telephone enquiries, took me to the Police Station in Hirschberg, where I found most of the rest of our party.

We had eight days in the Civil Prison (not a hotel this time!). Then I was taken back to Sagan. At first the camp authorities would not have me – said I must go back to the Police. We have since learned that those were Hitler's orders. However, the Sagan police chief made them take me; possibly he saved my life, and may have risked his own in doing so. After that I had fourteen days in the 'cooler' and then went back to normal camp life.

Appendix 2: Coincidences

As we have seen, Bernard Green was very fond of puns. The more dreadful the pun, the more he enjoyed it. One of his worst puns referred obliquely to his POW years.

'A man incarcerated in a prison cell was told by his captors that they would release him if he could invent a pun that would make them laugh. The man testily replied: "Oh pun the door", and walked out a free man.'

A pun is nothing more than a linguistic coincidence, an unlikely homonym that somehow tickles the funny bone. Green was very much a linguist, even though his German failed him in the freezing village of Boberöhrsdorf. He had a keen sense of irony and of the ridiculous and delighted in coincidences. He relished the fact that he had been taken prisoner near Skagen and eventually sent to Sagan.

During the writing and preparation of this book I have encountered a number of remarkable coincidences both in Bernard Green's experience and in my own.

In six German POW camps Green was bound to encounter a few RAF colleagues from early in the war. Dickens from Marlow was one, but the odds of meeting up with Major John Dodge, who had absolutely no Air Force connections, was remarkable.

In 1944 my uncle and aunt, Arthur and Peggy Faulkner, were sharing a house in Gloucestershire owned by Roger Bushell's mother. When the dire news of Bushell's murder on Hitler's orders arrived, my uncle and aunt had the impossible task of consoling Bushell's distraught mother and younger sister. Arthur Faulkner was my mother's older brother. In 1944 my father was a lieutenant in the Reconnaissance Corps preparing for the invasion of France in the Highlands of Scotland. He and my mother did not meet until 1945 and were married in 1948.

My cousin Penny, the daughter of Arthur and Peggy Faulkner, has another connection with Roger Bushell. Her godmother was Lady Georgina Curzon, a great friend and possible fiancée of Bushell's.

I was amazed to find that Hilary Walford, the lady who very ably and professionally edited this book, is a second cousin to Roger Bushell.

At the moment I don't seem to be able to get away from Bushell. Having just completed the editorial revisions for this book, I sat down to read a magazine called *An Baner Kernewek* (the *Cornish Flag*), for which I occasionally write. The first article I read was about a Battle of Britain Spitfire pilot who lives in Cornwall. After completing his training, he was posted to 92 Squadron commanded at the time by Squadron Leader Roger Bushell who was shot down a few days later.

Last and very much least is the fact concerning the actor Steve McQueen who played the spurious Virgil Hilts in the 1963 film *The Great Escape*, having insisted on the fictitious motorbike chase as the condition of his participation in the film. McQueen's birthday was 24 March, the date of the Great Escape.

Appendix 3

Intelligence Summary: 1st Buckinghamshire

Ploegsteert Wood in	1.5.15	Bn in trenches. Quiet day. 1 man killed early morning new breastwork (C Coy). Relieved by 5/Glosters 8.30 pm Bn marched back by platoons to billet in Romarin.
Romarin	2.5.15	Bn in billets. Divisional Reserve Romarin.
Romarin	3	----"----- -------"---------. 2 Coys on fatigue 6pm–3am in trenches of Warwick Brigade.
	4	----"----- ------"----------.
	5	----"----- ------"----------. Marched to trenches by platoons, took over from 5/Glosters 9pm. Sniping more lively than usual.
Ploegsteert Wood	6	Quiet morning, rifle grenades used on both sides. Two landed behind A Coy fire trench 4.15pm wounding Capts Reynolds, Bowyer, Lieut Green & 6 other ranks. 3 shells close to Bn HQ at 5pm. One man killed early morning (D Coy) in trench.

Appendix 4

Operations Record Book: No. 44 Squadron

RAF Form 540	
Waddington	**19th/20th July**
	"Gardening" Two aircraft successfully planted vegetables off SAMSO ISLAND, and two aircraft successfully planted vegetables off FREDERIKSHAVN. One aircraft failed to return, but is assumed to have planted its vegetable off FREDERIKSHAVN. The other four aircraft returned safely.

RAF Form 541

Aircraft Type and No.	Crew	Duty	Time Up	Time Down	Details of Sortie or Flight
L4087	Sgt E.L. Farrands Sgt P. Nixon. Sgt R. Miller P.O. B. Green. MC.	"Gardening"	20.46	????	Aircraft did not return to base. Wireless message received that aircraft forced landed in DENMARK. Assumed that vegetable successfully planted off FREDERIKSHAVN

Source: The National Archives – AIR 27/447

Appendix 5

The Fifty Victims and the Escapees

Flight Lieutenant **Henry J. Birkland**, Canadian, born 16 August 1917, 72 Squadron (shot down 7 November 1941, Spitfire Vb, W3367), recaptured near Sagan, last seen alive 31 March 1944; murdered by Lux and Scharpwinkel, cremated at Liegnitz.

Flight Lieutenant **E. Gordon Brettell** DFC, British, born 19 March 1915, 133 (Eagle) Squadron (shot down 26 September 1942, Spitfire IX BS313), recaptured Scheidemuhl; murdered by Bruchardt 29 March 1944, cremated at Danzig.

Flight Lieutenant **Lester G. Bull** DFC, British, born 7 November 1916, 109 Squadron (shot down 5/6 November 1941, Wellington IC, T2565), recaptured near Reichenberg; murdered 29 March 1944 by unknown Gestapo, cremated at Brux.

Squadron Leader **Roger J. Bushell**, South African born but in the regular RAF, born 30 August 1910, 92 Squadron (shot down 23 May 1940, Spitfire I, N3194), recaptured at Saarbrücken; murdered 29 March 1944 by Schulz, cremated at Saarbrücken.

Flight Lieutenant **Michael J. Casey**, British, born 19 February 1918, 57 Squadron (shot down 16 October 1939, Blenheim I, L1141), recaptured near Gorlitz; murdered 31 March 1944 by Lux and Scharpwinkel, cremated at Gorlitz.

Squadron Leader **James Catanach** DFC, Australian, born 28 November 1921, 455 (RAAF) Squadron (crash-landed in Norway, 6 September 1942, Hampden I AT109), recaptured at Flensburg; murdered 29 March 1944 by Post, cremated at Kiel.

Flight Lieutenant **Arnold G. Christensen**, New Zealander, born 8 April 1921, 26 Squadron (shot down in Mustang AL977 and POW 20 August 1942), recaptured at Flensburg; murdered 29 March 1944 by Post, cremated at Kiel.

Flying Officer **Dennis H. Cochran**, British, born 13 August 1921, 10 OTU (POW 9 November 1942), recaptured at Lorrach; murdered 31 March 1944 by Priess and Herberg, cremated at Natzweiler.

Squadron Leader **Ian K. P. Cross** DFC, British, born 4 April 1918, 103 Squadron (shot down 12 February 1942, Wellington IC, Z8714 PM:N), recaptured near Gorlitz; murdered 31 March 1944 by Lux and Scharpwinkel, cremated at Gorlitz.

Lieutenant **Halldor Espelid**, Norwegian, born 6 October 1920, 331 Squadron (shot down by flak 27 August 1942), Spitfire Vb BL588 FN:A east of Dunkirk, recaptured at Flensburg; murdered 29 March 1944 by Post, cremated at Kiel.

Flight Lieutenant **Brian H. Evans**, British, born 14 February 1920, 49 Squadron (shot down 6 December 1940), Hampden I, P4404 EA:R, recaptured at Halbau, last seen alive 31 March 1944; murdered by Lux and Scharpwinkel, cremated at Liegnitz.

Second Lieutenant **Nils Fuglesang**, Norwegian, 332 Squadron (shot down and belly landed in Holland, Spitfire IX BS540 AH:E, 2 May 1943), recaptured at Flensburg; murdered 29 March 1944 by Post, cremated at Kiel.

Lieutenant **Johannes S. Gouws**, South African, born 13 August 1919, 40 Squadron SAAF (shot down in Tomahawk AN377 and POW 9 April 1942), recaptured at Lindau; murdered 29 March 1944 by

Schneider, cremated at Munich.

Flight Lieutenant **William J. Grisman**, British, born 30 August 1914, 109 Squadron (believed shot down 5/6 November 1941, Wellington IC, T2565), recaptured near Gorlitz, last seen alive 6 April 1944; murdered by Lux, cremated at Breslau.

Flight Lieutenant **Alastair D. M. Gunn**, British, born 27 September 1919, 1 PRU (shot down in Spitfire PR.IV AA810 and POW 5 March 1942), recaptured near Gorlitz, last seen alive 6 April 1944; murdered by unknown Gestapo, cremated at Breslau.

Flight Lieutenant **Albert H. Hake**, Australian, born 30 June 1916, 72 Squadron (shot down 4 April 1942, Spitfire Vb AB258), recaptured near Gorlitz; murdered 31 March 1944 by Lux and Scharpwinkel, cremated at Gorlitz.

Flight Lieutenant **Charles P. Hall**, British, born 25 July 1918, 1 PRU (shot down in Spitfire AA804 and POW 28 December 1941), recaptured near Sagan; murdered 30 March 1944 by Lux and Scharpwinkel, cremated at Liegnitz.

Flight Lieutenant **Anthony R. H. Hayter**, British, born 20 May 1920, 148 Squadron (shot down in Wellington BB483 and POW 24 April 1942), recaptured near Mulhouse; murdered 6 April 1944 by Schimmel, cremated at Natzweiler.

Flight Lieutenant **Edgar S. Humphreys**, British, born 5 December 1914, 107 Squadron (shot down 19 December 1940, Blenheim IV, T1860), recaptured near Sagan, last seen alive 31 March 1944; murdered by Lux and Scharpwinkel, cremated at Liegnitz.

Flight Lieutenant **Gordon A. Kidder**, Canadian, born 9 December 1914, 156 Squadron (shot down 13/14 October 1942, Wellington III, BJ775), recaptured near Zlin; murdered 29 March 1944 by Zacharias and Knippelberg, with drivers Kiowsky and Schwartzer, cremated at Mahrisch Ostrau.

Flight Lieutenant **Reginald V. Kierath**, Australian, born 20 February 1915, 450 Squadron (shot down Kittyhawk III FR477 and POW 23 April 1943), recaptured near Reichenberg; murdered 29 March 1944 by unknown Gestapo, cremated at Brux.

Major **Antoni Kiewnarski**, Polish, born 26 January 1899, 305 Squadron (shot down 28 August 1942, Wellington X, Z1245), recaptured at Hirschberg; murdered there 31 March 1944 by Lux, place of cremation unknown.

Squadron Leader **Thomas G. Kirby-Green**, British, born 28 February 1918, 40 Squadron (shot down 16/17 October 1941, Wellington IC, Z8862 BL:B), recaptured near Zlin; murdered 29 March 1944 by Zacharias and Knippelberg, with drivers Kiowsky and Schwartzer, cremated at Mahrisch Ostrau.

Flying Officer **Wlodzimierz Kolanowski**, Polish, born 11 August 1913, 301 Squadron (shot down 8 November 1942, Wellington IV, Z1277 GR:Z), recaptured near Sagan; murdered at Liegnitz 31 March 1944 by Lux and Scharpwinkel, cremated at Liegnitz.

Flying Officer **Stanislaw Z. Krol**, Polish, born 22 March 1916, 74 Squadron (shot down 2 July 1941, Spitfire Vb, W3263), recaptured at Oels; murdered at Breslau 14 April 1944 probably by Lux, cremated at Breslau.

Flight Lieutenant **Patrick W Langford**, Canadian, born 4 November 1919, 16 OTU, (shot down 28/29 July 1942, Wellington IC, R1450), recaptured near Gorlitz, last seen alive 31 March 1944, murdered by Lux and Scharpwinkel, cremated at Liegnitz.

Flight Lieutenant **Thomas B. Leigh**, Australian in RAF, born 11 February 1919, 76 Squadron (shot down 5/6 August 1941, Halifax I, L9516), recaptured in Sagan area, last seen alive 12 April 1944; murdered by Lux and Scharpwinkel, cremated at Breslau.

Flight Lieutenant **James L. R. Long**, British, born 21 February 1915,

9 Squadron (shot down 27 March 1941, Wellington IA, R1335 WS:K), recaptured near Sagan, last seen alive 12 April 1944; murdered by Lux, cremated at Breslau.

Second Lieutenant **Clement A. N. McGarr**, South African, born 24 November 1917, 2 Squadron SAAF (shot down Tomahawk AK513 and POW 6 October 1941), recaptured near Sagan, last seen alive 6 April 1944; murdered by Lux, cremated at Breslau.

Flight Lieutenant **George E. McGill**, Canadian, born 14 April 1918, 103 Squadron (baled out of a damaged Wellington, R1192, 10/11 January 1942), recaptured in Sagan area, last seen alive 31 March 1944; murdered by Lux and Scharpwinkel; cremated at Liegnitz.

Flight Lieutenant **Romas Marcinkus**, Lithuanian, born 22 July 1910, 1 Squadron (shot down 12 February 1942, Hurricane IIc BD949 JX:J), recaptured at Scheidemuhl; murdered 29 March 1944 by Bruchardt, cremated at Danzig.

Flight Lieutenant **Harold J. Milford**, British, born 16 August 14, 226 Squadron (believed shot down Boston AL743 and POW 22 September 1942), recaptured near Sagan, last seen alive 6 April 1944; murdered by Lux, cremated at Breslau.

Flying Officer **Jerzy Tomasc Mondschein**, Polish, born 18 March 1909, 304 Squadron (shot down 8 November 1941, Wellington IC, R1215), recaptured in Reichenberg area; murdered Brux 29 March 1944 by unknown Gestapo, cremated at Brux.

Flying Officer **Kazimierz Pawluk**, Polish, born 1 July 1906, 305 Squadron (shot down 29 March 1942, Wellington II, W5567 SM:M), recaptured at Hirschberg; murdered there on 31 March 1944 by Lux, place of cremation unknown.

Flight Lieutenant **Henri A. Picard** Croix de Guerre, Belgian, born 17 April 1916, 350 Squadron (shot down Spitfire BM297 and POW 2 September 1942), recaptured at Scheidemuhl; murdered 29 March

1944 by Bruchardt, cremated at Danzig.

Flying Officer **John P. P. Pohe**, New Zealander, born 10 December 1921, 51 Squadron (shot down 22/23 September 1943, Halifax II, JN901), recaptured near Gorlitz; murdered 31 March 1944 by Lux and Scharpwinkel, cremated at Gorlitz. Also known by his Maori name of Porokoru Patapu.

Sous-Lieutenant **Bernard W. M. Scheidhauer**, French, born 28 August 1921, 131 Squadron (ran low on fuel and landed by mistake on Jersey, 18 November 1942, Spitfire Vb EN830 NX:X), recaptured at Saarbrücken; murdered 29 March 1944 by Spann, cremated at Saarbrücken.

Pilot Officer **Sotiris Skanzikas**, Greek, born 6 August 1921, 336 Squadron (shot down Hurricane HW250 and POW 23 July 1943), recaptured at Hirschberg; murdered 30 March 1944 by Lux, place of cremation unknown.

Lieutenant **Rupert J. Stevens**, South African, born 21 February 1919, 12 Squadron SAAF (shot down in Martin Maryland AH287 and POW 14 November 1941), recaptured at Rosenheim; murdered 29 March 1944 by Schneider, cremated at Munich.

Flying Officer **Robert C. Stewart**, British, born 7 July 1911, 77 Squadron (shot down 26/27 April 1943, Halifax II, DT796), recaptured near Sagan, last seen alive 31 March 1944; murdered by Lux and Scharpwinkel, cremated at Liegnitz.

Flight Lieutenant **John G. Stower**, British, born 15 September 1916, 142 Squadron (shot down 16/17 November 1942, Wellington III, BK278, QT:C), recaptured near Reichenberg; murdered 31 March 1944 by unknown Gestapo, place of cremation unknown.

Flight Lieutenant **Denys O. Street**, British, born 1 April 1922, 207 Squadron (shot down 29/30 March 1943, Lancaster I, EM:O), recaptured near Sagan, last seen alive 6 April 1944; murdered by Lux;

cremated at Breslau. Street is the only victim whose ashes are not at Poznan; his rest at the Berlin 1939–1945 War Cemetery.

Flight Lieutenant **Cyril D. Swain**, British, born 15 December 1911, 105 Squadron (shot down 28 November 1940, Blenheim IV, T1893), recaptured near Gorlitz, last seen alive 31 March 1944; murdered by Lux and Scharpwinkel, cremated at Liegnitz.

Flying Officer **Pawel W. Tobolski**, Polish, born 21 March 1906, 301 Squadron (shot down 25/26 June 1942, Wellington IV Z1479, GR:A), recaptured at Stettin; murdered at Breslau 2 April 1944 probably by Lux, cremated at Breslau.

Flight Lieutenant **Arnost Valenta**, Czech, born 25 October 1912, 311 Squadron (shot down 6 February 1941, Wellington IC, L7842 KX:T), recaptured near Gorlitz, last seen alive 31 March 1944; murdered by Lux and Scharpwinkel; cremated at Liegnitz.

Flight Lieutenant **Gilbert W. Walenn**, British, born 24 February 1916, 25 OTU (shot down Wellington N2805 and POW 11 September 1941), recaptured at Scheidemuhl; murdered 29 March 1944 by Bruchardt, cremated at Danzig.

Flight Lieutenant **James C. Wernham**, Canadian, born 15 January 1917, 405 Squadron (shot down 8/9 June 1942, Halifax II, W7708 LQ:H), recaptured at Hirschberg; murdered 31 March 1944 by Lux, place of cremation unknown.

Flight Lieutenant **George W. Wiley**, Canadian, born 24 January 1922, 112 Squadron (shot down Kittyhawk III 245788 and POW 12 March 1943), recaptured near Gorlitz; murdered 31 March 1944 by Lux and Scharpwinkel, cremated at Gorlitz.

Squadron Leader **John E. A. Williams** DFC, Australian in RAF, born 6 May 1919, 450 Squadron (shot down Kittyhawk III FR270 and POW 31 October 1942), recaptured near Reichenberg; murdered 29 March 1944 by Lux, cremated at Brux.

Flight Lieutenant **John F. Williams**, British, born 7 July 1917, 107 Squadron (shot down 27 April 1942, Boston III Z2194), recaptured near Sagan, last seen alive 6 April 1944; murdered by unknown Gestapo, cremated at Breslau.

Recaptured and returned to captivity

Returned to Sagan

Flight Lieutenant **Albert Armstrong** (268 Squadron).

Flight Lieutenant **R. Anthony Bethell** (268 Squadron, shot down near Alkmaar, 7 December 1942, Mustang AP212 'V', born 9 April 1922).

Flight Lieutenant **Leslie Charles James Brodrick** (106 Squadron, shot down Stuttgart, 14/15 April 1943, Lancaster ED752 ZN:H, born May 1921).

Flying Officer **William J. Cameron** (RCAF).

Flight Lieutenant **Richard Sidney Albion Churchill** (144 Squadron, born 1918).

Flight Lieutenant **Bernard 'Pop' Green** (44 Squadron, shot down 19/20 July 1940, Hampden I L4087).

Flight Lieutenant **Roy Brouard Langlois** (12 Squadron, shot down 5 August 1941, Wellington II, W5421 PH:G).

Flight Lieutenant **Robert McBride**.

Flight Lieutenant **Alistair Thompson McDonald**.

Flight Lieutenant **Henry Cuthbert 'Johnny' Marshall**.

Lieutenant **Alexander Desmond Neely** (825 Squadron Fleet Air Arm, shot down near Dunkirk in May 1940, born November 1917).

Flight Lieutenant **Thomas Robert Nelson** (37 Squadron, born March 1915).

Flight Lieutenant **Alfred Keith Ogilvie** DFC (Canadian, 609 Squadron, born March 1915).

Lieutenant **Douglas Arthur Poynter** (Fleet Air Arm, born 1921).

Flight Lieutenant **Laurence Reavell-Carter** (49 Squadron).

Flight Lieutenant **Paul Gordon Royle** (53 Squadron RAAF).

Flight Lieutenant **Michael Moray Shand** (485 Squadron RNZAF, born 18 March 1915).

Flight Lieutenant **Alfred Burke Thompson** (102 Squadron, shot down 8/9 September 1939, Whitley III, K8950).

Squadron Leader **Leonard Henry Trent** VC (487 Squadron, shot down 3 May 1943, Ventura II AJ209, EG:G).

Recaptured and taken to Sachsenhausen, later returned to Stalag Luft III, Sagan

Flight Lieutenant **Ray van Wymeersch** (174 Squadron Free French Air Force, born September 1920, shot down 19 August 42, Hurricane IIc BP299 'U').

Recaptured and sent to Stalag Luft I, Barth

Flight Lieutenant **Desmond Lancelot Plunkett** (Rhodesian, 218 Squadron, shot down Emden 20/21 June 1942, Stirling I W7530, HA:Q, born February 1915).

Recaptured and sent to Oflag IVC, Colditz Castle

Flight Lieutenant **Bedrich Dvorak** (312 Squadron, shot down by FW 190 of JG 2 on 3 June 1942 near Cherbourg in Spitfire VB, BL340, DU:X, born 1912).

Flight Lieutenant **Ivor B. Tonder** (Czech, 312 Squadron, born April 1913, shot down on 3 June 1942 by FW 190 of JG 2 over Channel close by Cherbourg in Spitfire VB, BL626, DU:I).

Recaptured, sent to Sachsenhausen and later reached safety
Wing Commander **Harry Melville Arbuthnot 'Wings' Day** AM (converted to GC in 1971) DSO OBE.

Major **Johnnie Dodge** DSO DSC MC. Repatriated by the Germans via Switzerland, in order to negotiate peace terms with Winston Churchill.

Flight Lieutenant **Sydney Henstings Dowse** MC (PRU, born 21 November 1918).

Flight Lieutenant **Bertram Arthur James** MC (9 Squadron, shot down Duisburg 5/6 June 1940, Wellington IA P9232 WS:M, born April 1915).

Evaded recapture and escaped to England
Flight Lieutenant **Per** (or **Peter**) **Bergsland** (Norwegian, 332 Squadron, shot down 19 August 1942, Spitfire Vb AB269, born 17 January 1919) and Flight Lieutenant **Jens Muller** (Norwegian, 331 Squadron) reached England via Stettin and Sweden.

Flight Lieutenant **Bob van der Stok** (or **Vanderstok**) (Dutch, 41 Squadron, shot down 12 April 1942, Spitfire Vb BL595, born 13 October 1915) reached England via Spain.

(Details of the Great Escapers based upon research carried out by Rob Davis and reproduced with kind permission.)

Appendix 6: 'My Dear Adrian…'

What follows is the complete correspondence from Bernard Green (my grandfather) to his son Adrian Green (my father) from 6 August 1940 to 30 December 1944 from five POW camps in Germany and Poland. Each letter and postcard was carefully read, reread and carried for months in Adrian's battledress pockets to be carefully put in order and stored in a brown envelope after the end of the war.

Through the letters and postcards we may trace Adrian's wartime service: from private in his father's old regiment the Ox. and Bucks Light Infantry, to failed OCTU candidate, to Lance Corporal in the Ox. and Bucks in Northern Ireland, to successful Officer Cadet at Sandhurst, and to Second Lieutenant, Lieutenant and Captain in the newly formed Reconnaissance Corps in the Highlands of Scotland, Normandy, Belgium, the Netherlands and finally Germany. We see that the correspondence, neatly addressed to 'Cortegar, Bourne End, Bucks' is redirected to Adrian Green in his mother's handwriting, the rank and regiments changing as the war progressed.

These are fond and considerate letters written by a man who, in many ways, often found writing easier than words. There is not a trace of self-pity in any of the letters; plenty of reassurance and hope that the war would soon be over. There is much gentle irony; references to struggles with various foreign languages, the recording of coincidences, and the observation that playing hockey was not for him. There is no bitterness; Bernard Green tacitly admits that he had chosen to leave a comfortable life beside the Thames to fly against a ruthless enemy. There are only two references to his wife Dorothea (referred to as D) with whom twenty-five years of marriage were turning increasingly sour.

For obvious reasons I have not included the numerous letters Bernard wrote to his friend Evelyn Haberer, the lady he married after the death in 1951 of Dorothea. They are outside the scope of this book and have no real bearing on the story of his part in the Great Escape from Stalag Luft III. He must, however, have been sustained by this friendship during the long years of imprisonment as he was by the constant letters from Adrian and the sporadic ones from Dorothea and his daughter Catherine (referred to as C).

The matter-of-fact tone of the letters occasionally gives way to somewhat poetic observations. He refers to the 'very fine cloud effects' in the Baltic summer at Barth and gives Adrian some sound advice on his fleeting engagement to a woman referred to as JM whom he met while stationed in Scotland. He constantly emphasises the fact that he is fit and delights in the small pleasures of camp life: cigarettes, bread pudding, warm clothes and good company.

After his postcard written the day of the escape, 24 March 1944, there is a marked concentration on theatrical productions. His letter of 25 April 1944 contains no reference to his escape, capture and unpleasant eight days in a police cell followed by two weeks' solitary confinement in the 'cooler'. There is only an oblique possible reference to the murder of Roger Bushell; anything more blatant would never have passed the German censors.

The last postcard, sent on 30 December 1944, sets the scene for the gruelling 'Black March', which began three weeks later. It ends on a very positive note; 'All the very best – Here's to our meeting next year. BG.'

(Note: The letters have been transcribed exactly as they were written, including punctuation and spelling mistakes.)

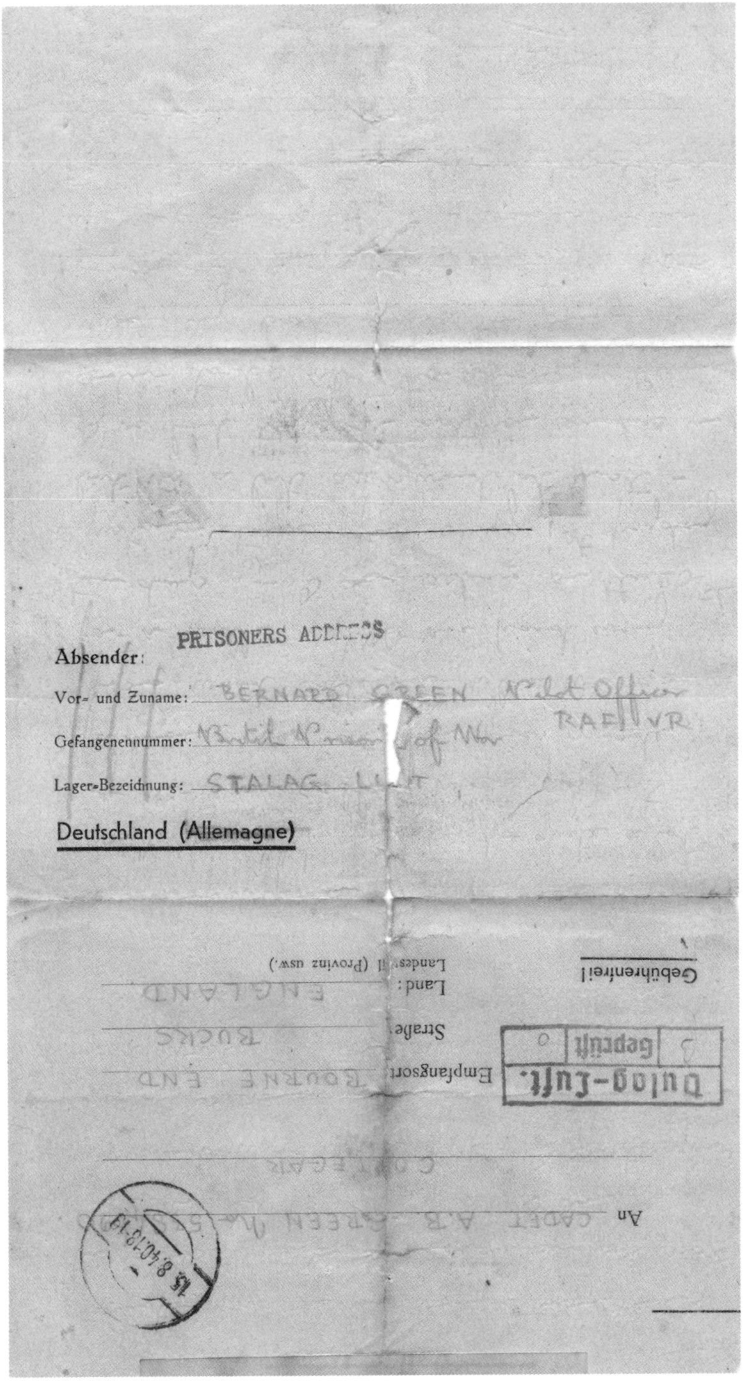
PRISONERS ADDRESS

Absender:

Vor- und Zuname: BERNARD GREEN Pilot Officer RAF VR

Gefangenennummer: Brit. Prisoner of War

Lager-Bezeichnung: STALAG LUFT

Deutschland (Allemagne)

Gebührenfrei!

Dulag-Luft. Geprüft

An CADET A. B. GREEN

Empfangsort: BOURNE END

Straße: BUCKS

Land: ENGLAND

Landesteil (Provinz usw.)

15.8.40.-18-19

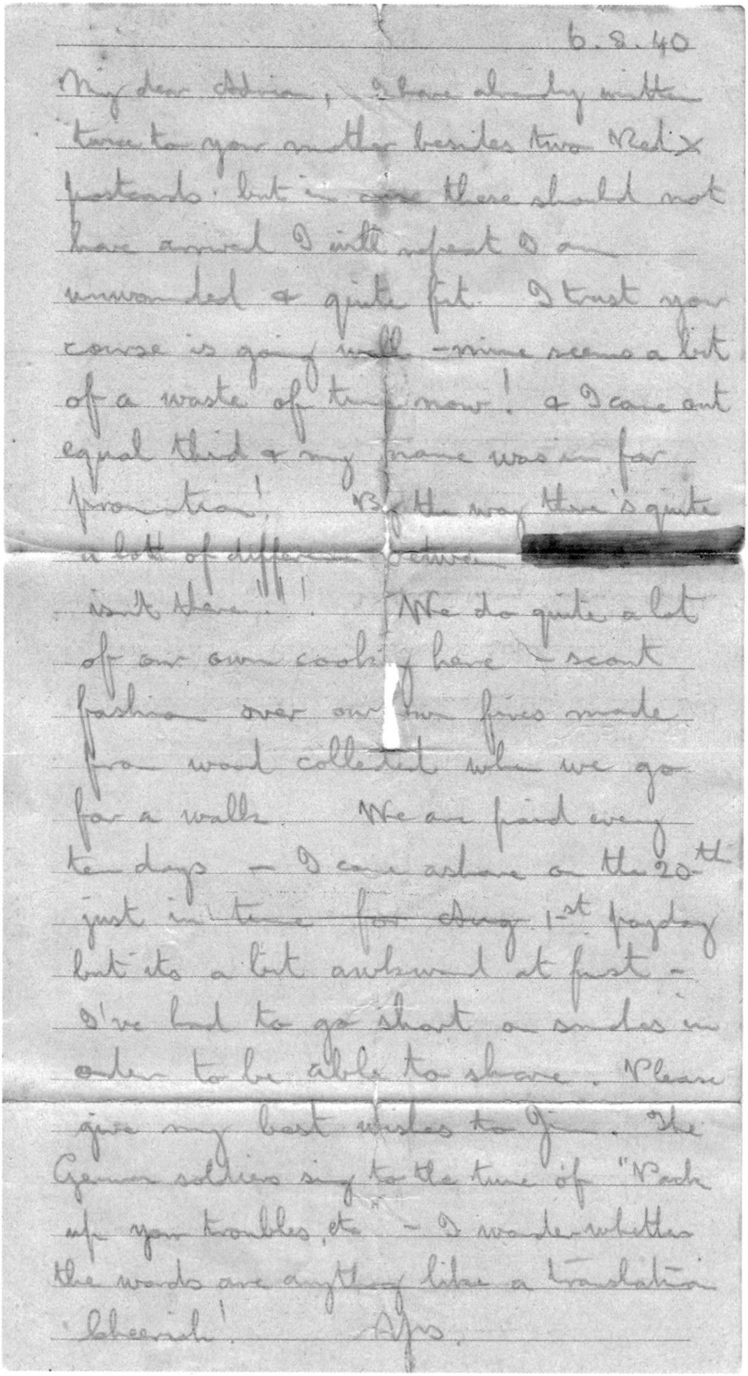

6.8.40

My dear Adrian, I have already written twice to you another besides two Red X postcards but in case these should not have arrived I will repeat I am unwounded & quite fit. I trust your course is going well — mine seems a bit of a waste of time now! & I came out equal third & my name was in for promotion! By the way there's quite a lot of difference between [redacted] isn't there!!! We do quite a lot of our own cooking here — scout fashion over our own fires made from wood collected when we go for a walk. We are paid every ten days — I came ashore on the 20th just in time for Aug 1st payday but its a bit awkward at first — I've had to go short on smokes in order to be able to shave. Please give my best wishes to Jim. The German soldiers sing to the tune of "Pack up your troubles, etc" — I wonder whether the words are anything like a translation.

Cheerioh!

Ajs.

6.8.40 [Letter]

My dear Adrian. I have already written twice to your mother besides two Red X postcards but in case these should not have arrived I will repeat I am unwounded & quite fit. I trust your course is going well – mine seems a bit of a waste of time now! & I came out equal third & my name was up for promotion! By the way there is quite a bit of difference between [BLACKED OUT] *isn't there!!! We do quite a lot of our own cooking here – scout fashion over our own fires made from wood collected when we go for a walk. We are paid every ten days – I came ashore on the 20th – just in time for Aug 1st payday but it's a bit awkward at first – I've had to go short on smokes in order to be able to share. Please give my best wishes to Jim. The German soldiers sing to the tune of 'Pack up your troubles, etc' – I wonder whether the words are anything like a translation.*
Cheerioh! Yrs.

7.10.40 [Letter]

My dear Adrian. This is to wish you very many happy returns of the day as this letter may take all that time to reach you. The two men I'm sharing a room with are both 21 this month – one of them today. I'm hoping you will have got your commission by now. Our compound has been enlarged & is now about 1/4 mile round. Have had a few Red X parcels through – it was great having tea again & English cigarettes. Am getting quite a dab at rolling cigs – the German machine is definitely good & one's camp money goes much further that way. We get very little news here except from fresh officers – you can imagine how interesting it is when a new batch comes in & you spot people you know. If you are still with Jim tell him Dickens is here – his house is next door to the Buckmasters! & theres a man who went up to London & back by my trains! & another who has a summer bungalow at Marlow – the S/L knows W/C Page
yrs, BG

1.12.40 [Letter]

My dear Adrian. I am writing this on your 21st b-day tho' it will have to go next month. It is a Friday & you were born on a Friday – curious but I suppose it depends on the number of Leap Years in between. Here's wishing you very many happier returns of the day. Have had no letters from England yet but I expect you have had your commission for some time now & have probably heard from me. Life goes on much the same here except that we are rather short of cigarettes! Have had a pc from the BL in Geneva so shall probably be getting some from them shortly.

We get an extraordinary amount of sunshine in the winter here – 4/5 hours average per day with some very fine cloud effects – the effect I suppose of getting well away from the Gulf Stream.
With love to everyone
Yrs, BG

25.2.41 [Postcard]
Very many thanks for letter received 31/1/41 – regret not possible reply more fully. A man called Carr here has brother acting local theatre – perhaps you have seen him – Carr acted in 10 minute alibi here. Glad to hear Bertie is now director T&G – will be good thing for you. Have got nucleus of band here – concert in 3 weeks. All very best, BG

28.4.41 [Postcard]
Many thanks yrs 29/11/40 & 16/12/40 received 25/4/41! by same post 29/1/41 & 17/12/41 from KOG – writing her next month early. Glad to hear boat OK. Letter [unclear] *received 8/4/41 – wrote agreeing your choice. Glad to hear bun shop etc is still there! Am the recognised authority on bread pudding – do one nearly every night. One keeps very fit – Red X food arriving regularly. Love to all. BG*

27.7.41 [Postcard]
V.many thanks yrs of 19/1/41 & 28/2/41 recd 29/4/41 & 7/7/41. I had a charming letter from Lorna M also from HD. We had "10 minute Alibi" here – Dickens from Marlow was the police Sgt – also our sgts here did "Journeys End" damn well – strange seeing it again here! Glad to hear you are flourishing – 14 stone I hear! Am v fit – cig & food parcels coming thro' well. Every good wish, BG.

28.9.41 [Postcard]
V.many thanks for yrs of 18/5/41, 16/6/41 & 20/7/41 recd 8/9/41, 28/8/41 & 17/9/41 respectively. Am hoping to manage letter with photo next month. Please thank Lorna M for hers 1/7/41 recd 17/9/41 – hope pc next month. Hope I shall be able play "Robbers March"! Have now got khaki trousers (with 5 pockets!) & khaki great coat – great treat! I take in a German newspaper regularly. Am quite fit – trust you are. All the best, BG.

7.10.41 [Letter]

My dear Adrian. I expect this letter will arrive round about yr birthday, so here's wishing you v many happy returns of the day. Read yrs of 21/8/41 on 1/10/41 – v many thanks. Photo was taken last April. My love & v best wishes to Lorna M. for 21st – got her letter 17/9/41 – v m thanks – hope p.c. soon. Interested to hear about mill. Am doing lot of reading – have now many books & we write our names inside cover of other peoples books & they come round in due course – am picking up with all reading one hadn't time for before. Also reading French, German & Spanish – Spanish is chief difficulty – am hoping to get hold of Spanish–German dictionary as nearest I can get – good practice anyway! How are you getting on about your commission? We get lot of sun this time of year – this seems the best month & August about the worst! Have been playing lot of chess – pocket set v. useful – extraordinary how one's brain gets more active thro' having more opportunities of using it. The winter session of the "Stalag University" started yesterday – people take courses for permanent commissions, navigation & even the BSc! Hope things are going well with you – I hear you are getting quite plump! We have a nephew of Holley's (the grand man) here called Saville – knows Flackwell Heath quite well & my batman (Holloway) knows Percy Easton! Heartiest good wishes – keep your spirits up! Yrs, BG.

14.12.41 [Postcard]

My dear A. V.m. thanks yrs of 14/9 (recd 28/10). Congrats on [unclear] *stripe! am hoping you will pull off comm.. Yes we got bathing during summer – on Xmas day shall have been here 17 months. Red X parcels excellent – am getting fat! Am finding Russia a bit on top side but am plugging away! We are clearing ground to make skating rink round hydrant but it will prob only be sliding – no skates! All v. best, BG.*

16.1.42 [Postcard]

My dear Adrian, V. many thanks for yrs of 18/10 & 2/11 – they take abt 2 months to come. Yes, I was v.glad to hear of C's engagement. I wonder whether it wd amuse you if you are near enough to look up the Cowans at Clady Cottage, Dunadry – Miss C was my governess. Yes I remember F. Rowe quite well – Carr (who was here) had a brother in the cast for some time. V. many thanks for b'day wishes – happy NY to you! C wd choose the Marlow D! Have part of compound flooded for skating. We are v. cheery & optimistic here. Am v. fit & trust you are. Sorry letter imposs. All v.best, BG.

6.3.42 [Letter]

My dear A, V.m. thanks for yrs of 28/11, 13/12 & 25/12 recd 29/1, 7/2 & 22/1 respectively. Its great of you to write so often, am v interested to hear how things are going with you. Its excellent that the light boat is still in good condition – am looking forward to a trip myself in another year or so! V.m. thanks for the cig base for Silver Wedding – another thing to look forward to using – also for tobacco via BAT – Red X food parcels come thro' regularly but all others hung up for some time – expect they will come thro' in a lump. Manage to get at least 1/2 hr skating each day now – just had cold snap – down to -13°C in day time + strong NE er – wonder what Chas K wd say to that! our "odes" are rather different to his! P/O M'Comb not here but will keep look out for him – we had a Squadron leader M'Comb here up to last summer – possibly a relative? Yes I had heard that Lorna is now a Wren – I should think the uniform suits her doesn't it? We've had plenty of snow hanging about here for some time now – piled up to 6 ft in some places round skating rink – a useful buffer for ice hockey – but its getting rather dirty & there'll be an awful mess when it thaws – when wind blows visibility abt 100 yds. With every good wish, Yrs, BG

14.6.42 [Letter]

My dear A. Very many thanks for yours of 28/2, 24/6, 6/4, 25/4, & 12/5 – the last took just over 3 weeks – I am very interested & very much appreciate your frequent letters. Lorna M asked for snap – would you please send her enclosed. Through good offices of one of the Canadians have had USA food parcel from Hollywood – very nice too! – maple syrup! Very glad to hear you are going to OCTU & hope it has now come off. Was immensely pleased with photos of C & you which your mother sent. Poor old D! – I'm sorry – yes its about 2 _ years since we were there. Very sorry not to be at wedding – the letters got mixed up & deduced that C was married on reading that your mother was helping her in the housekeeping! but got other letter soon after. Dickens of Marlow tells me it was quite local sensation. Thanks so much for acting for me – hear you did it very well – grand that weather was fine. We have double summer time 2 hours ahead of German time & 3 hours ahead of the sun! Yes have heard from MHP. Will be grand to have wedding photos. Good idea selling boat. No walks here but better "circus". We now have 6 in the room but plenty of room. Have got cricket gear & pitch not bad – but not for me! Am very fit & trust you are. Parcels OK – including plenty of smokes – got clothing one with attaché case on 2/6/42. Best of luck – we certainly seem to be getting in sight of end of war. Your affec. father, BG

27.8.42 [Letter]

My dear Adrian

Very many thanks for yours of 5/6 & 18/7 & for congrats – the Germans don't recognise any post capture promotion – quite useful as one can save money being only paid here on P/O basis. Capital of Trust Deed is 500 ordinary shares in T&G – you will find copy of deed under T in concertina file in my desk. Like this camp better than last – more elbow room – less dust – washing arrangements rather limited but shall probably be moved again before Xmas. Trust you have been posted by now – must be trying having to wait – glad to hear you've been selected – seems to be very thorough. Get German newspapers regularly – otherwise only get news from the "new boys". Please thank you mother for hers of 22/5 (received 24/8!) & 2/8 & C for hers of 16/6 – have spoken to S L Davie only this morning. I would like 3 prs aertex pants preferably with elastic belts please – have plenty of vests. Glad to hear you are fit – same here. Very hot lately – over 100 in shade some days – one dresses by putting on shorts on place of bathing slips! Band is giving pretty good shows – part of side of canteen removed & audience can sit in open. There is a man here whose uncle was my closest friend at Clifton & another from Lymington. I wonder whether C has seen the Blakes lately!! Like wedding photos very much. All the very best, yrs, BG.

1.11.42 [Letter]

My dear A, Very many thanks for yours of 27/7, 8/8, 6/9 & 19/9. Very many happy returns for the 29th! Very interested to hear you are now well on the way to a commission. Yes I remember Olga FW quite well. Thanks for sending photo on to LM. I thought this impression of my studying Russian by a room mate might amuse you. Not much chance of getting snaps taken here but may get copy of the official one taken for identification. Yes, all parcels arriving well except books but have got some excellent German ones through the canteen. As you will have heard this is an entirely different camp although address is SL3 as before for letters.

We are having splendid weather & it is great having a number of deciduous trees all round us & good view of the surrounding country – the camp is known as Oflag XXI.B. Please tell your mother I would be very grateful if she would thank the Group Captain for a further 500 Players (BAT 61040) Am very fit & glad my latest news is the same for all 3 of you. Glad to hear you were able to meet Jim – congrats on 2nd pip. Lectures here are pretty good – am even beginning to know a little history! but we haven't got concerts etc organised yet. All the very best, yrs BG

29.11.42 [Postcard]

My dear A, Very many thanks for yours of 6/10 & 13/10 – also many happy returns of today! Congrats on being posted – fairly near home too – brings up memories of Bertram Mills! Yes. the X red parcels are pretty good spec. the Canadian ones. Snow seems to have settled in here for the winter now. Am very fit & trust you continue so. Have now started Italian – seems easier than most languages. Every good wish, BG.

31.1.43 [Postcard]

My dear A, Thanks very much for yours of 25/10 – in spite of "blue pencil" I know where you are. You must find it good after so long in barrack rooms etc – I also have struck it lucky – am in a moderately comfortable room with 3 Wing Commanders – 2 of them newly married! Yes, am very fit – so sorry letter not possible yet. Everyone here in good spirits. All very best. BG

28.2.43 [Postcard]

My dear A, Thanks very much for yours of 25/11 & 3/1. We were very interested to hear about opening of the bridge. Yes I remember the doll quite well – my love to L. Congrats to Trevor. Are you still in the infantry? Am reading Gone with the Wind – every sentence is interesting – also getting on quite well with Don Quijote in the Spanish. Trust you keep fit "as this leaves me at present". All the very best, BG.

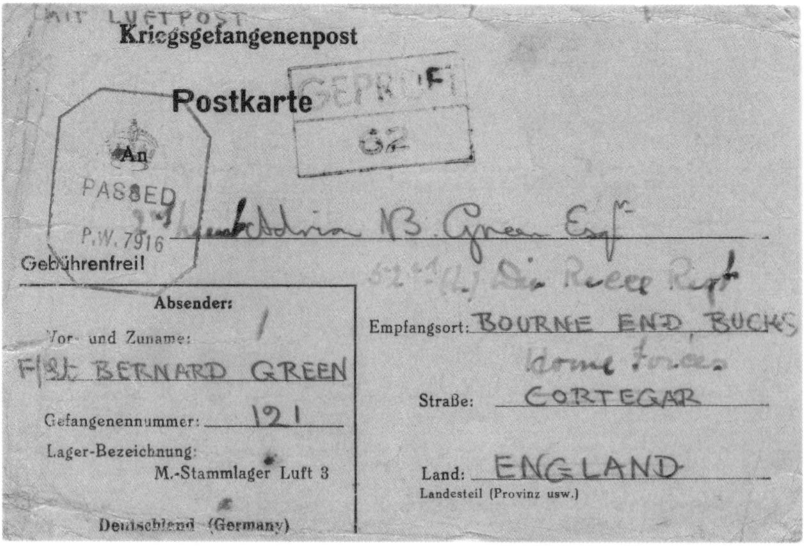

23.3.43 [Letter]

My dear A, Very many thanks for yours of 6/12 & 14/1. Was very interested to get the photo – its good of you & the whole crew look pretty useful. What was the name of the man whose father was on the MGTC course? Major Dodge, who is here, was also on the same course. Your letter of 14/1 suffered considerably at the hands of the censor! Congrats to Trevor! Am now reading "The Sun is my Undoing" – I wonder whether you know it – an extremely virile & interesting book – haven't found out yet who sent it to me. herewith photo – you will see I'm finding a use still for the old black buttoned jacket! This is the best time of the year – warmer weather with plenty of sun & the flies haven't started yet – the only nuisance is the dust as we get fairly consistent strong winds. Have had news of one of the Vineys being at the prison camp from which my 3 room mates come – one of them lives at Cookham on the hill just above the fire station & Ayres, the orderly who does my washing comes from Marlow – we swop local news occasionally. Have you any news of Maybury? I often remember the time when we had sauerkraut at Manchester – we get plenty here but it isn't cooked in quite the same way! Am very fit & hope you are. Just completed 32 months as POW. All the very best, yrs, BG

28.4.43 [Postcard]

My dear A, Very many thanks for yours of 15/2 – glad to hear things are going well with you. Red X food comes through well & have just had another food parcel from Hollywood! Am very fit & hope you are. Back at SL3 but in new compound

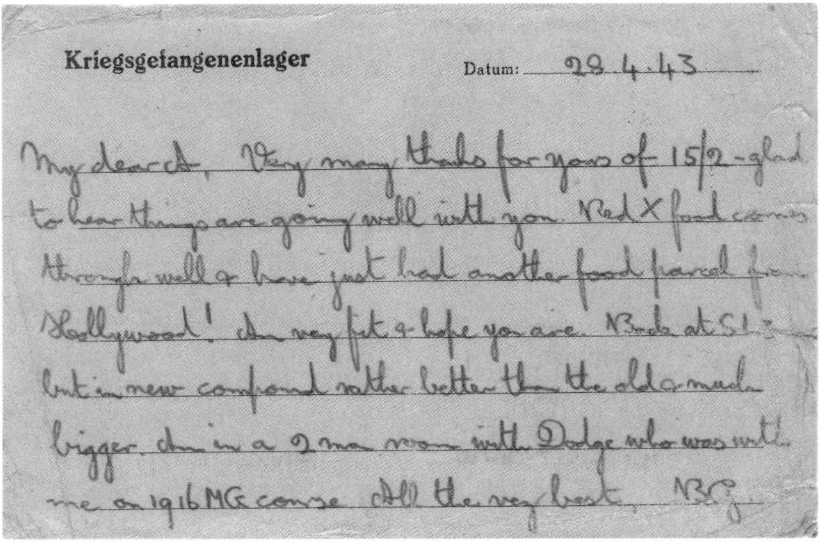
Kriegsgefangenenlager Datum: 28.4.43

My dear A, Very many thanks for yours of 15/2 - glad to hear things are going well with you. Red X food comes through well & have just had another food parcel from Hollywood! Am very fit & hope you are. Back at SL3 but in new compound rather better than the old & much bigger. Am in a 2 man room with Dodge who was with me on 1916 MG course. All the very best, BG *rather better than the old & much bigger. Am in a 2 man room with Dodge who was with me on 1916 MG course. All the very best. BG.*

3.6.43 [Letter]

My dear Adrian

Very many thanks for yours of 20/3, 29/3 & 7/4. So glad to hear about your commission & your mother & C being able to come – good to be posted along with chaps you know. Trust you are fit as I am. Interested to hear of Maybury – have often enquired whether he was over here from men from the batallion. Mail gets through rather more quickly now. The same apparatus that you saw in the film is quite a familiar sight to us too! Shall look forward to seeing the film "Queen Victoria" – liked the other 2 immensely. Had a parade for the King's birthday today – incidentally its what the Germans call "Himmelfahrt". Unfortunately I can't remember the charabanc incident. Am playing a lot of chess – 3 or 4 games a day. Had a letter from Hugh D recently with quite a lot of interesting news. Been reading "Green Grows the City" – like B Nichols sense of humour immensely.

Camp beginning to look like a red Indian reservation, bathing slips being the usual attire! Had a chat with a relative of the Myrings (Petley) recently. I see its Davids second birthday as a POW a few days ago – Lorna has been able to send a cable but hasn't heard from him yet. All the very best – take care of yourself. Your affect father, BG.

1.8.43 [Letter]

My dear A, Very many thanks for yours of 18/4, 2/5, 9/5, 29/5, 16/6 & 1/7. It is splendid of you to write so often & so interestingly. We also have been having great weather – strong sun with cooling breezes. I hope your leave at BE with JM was a great success – shame missing T's wedding – I bet S was in great form! I ran across an ex MG sgt in a printing works at Reading some time ago – can't remember his name – your mention of Butler & Tanner reminded me – couldn't be same man I suppose? Yes am starting 4th year now – looks as though it might be the last. Very interested to hear all about JM & to hear you are looking ahead – in these days, thank goodness, we do realise that the first "fine careless rapture" is bound to modify itself & I am very glad to think that you are visualising that & asking yourself whether the ingredients are there for a development into something calmer but perhaps even deeper & finer.

Personally I have a prejudice for Scotswomen as wives, not on the well worn humorous reference to thrift but from observation of general all round qualities.

Enjoyed reading "John Baxter, Bookseller" very much. The RC sounds very interesting – not much information from POW's but I get general idea. Which Jack is it in 8th Army? Very well, trust you are. Every good wish and congrats. BG.

3.10.43 [Letter]
My dearest A, Very many thanks for yours of 24/7, 13/8 & 10/9 – much appreciated. Would you please ask your mother to include in next parcel pr of trousers, khaki or RAF battle dress, khaki preferred – per Simpsons. Hope all effects of tonsillitis have passed off – am very fit. Very little of your letters get censured. Yes, news is good but it seems slow to us! Half expected your news re JM – hope it doesn't hurt too much. We have our own bugle calls for roll call here – played on a cornet – sometimes varied with other tunes – "On a cold & frosty morning", when you're expecting 102 in shade! We had "George & Margaret" in the theatre (built by POWs rather on lines of BE cinema but of wood) last week – extremely well done – next week we have having N. Coward's "Design for Living" & after that "Rookery Nook". So the 15 buses are still running! No. I hadn't heard about Cliveden Woods – great scheme – I suppose we shall be able to picnic there.
We have an exchange & mart known as "Foodacco" – put in what you don't want & credited with points & take out equivalent value in points of what you do want – very useful. Heaps of thanks for letter & all the best. BG.

7.12.43 [Postcard]
My dear A, Many happy returns of 29/11 & also all the very best for Xmas & the New Year. Am very fit & hope you are. Just had a play written by a POW here – "Twinkle, twinkle Wm Starr" – damn good – a great success. We are spreading ourselves on Xmas as we all expect it to be our last as POWs. All the best. BG.

24.3.44 [Postcard – the day of the Great Escape]
My dear A, Heaps of thanks for yours of 5/12, 12/12 & 7/1. Tough being away for Xmas – here we had quite a reasonable one – Red X did us very well. Congrats on 2nd pip! quick work. Yes, I believe it was Stone. Clive blue pencilled except for de-motion! Am very fit but rather tired of snow & slush. All the very best, yrs. BG.

25.4.44 [Letter]
My dear A, Very many thanks for yours of 5/12, 12/2 & 7/1. Please wish your mother very many happies of 7/5 from me. Yes, I can imagine Clive's locker! Hope he's OK now, give him my paternal blessing if you're writing. Am now in a room

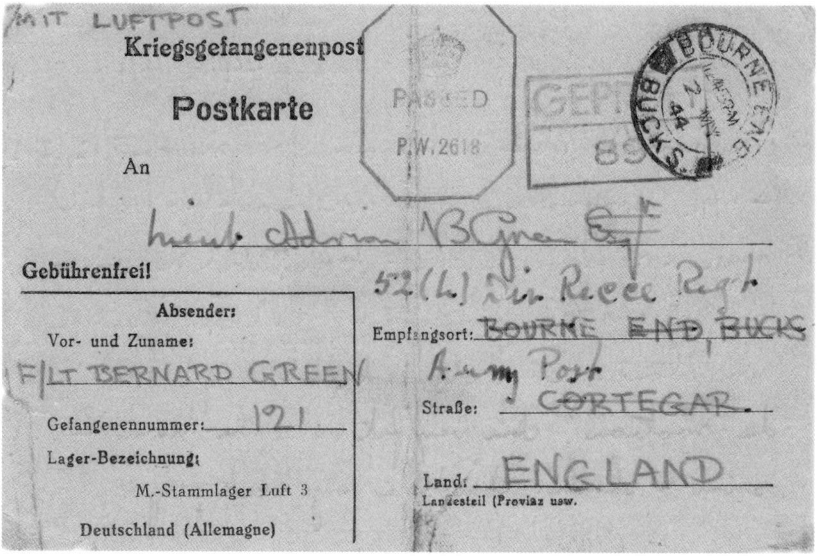
MIT LUFTPOST

Kriegsgefangenenpost

Postkarte

PASSED
P.W. 2618

BOURNE END BUCKS
2 MY 44

An

Lieut Adrian B Green Esq

Gebührenfrei!

Absender:
Vor- und Zuname: F/LT BERNARD GREEN
Gefangenennummer: 121
Lager-Bezeichnung:
M.-Stammlager Luft 3
Deutschland (Allemagne)

52 (L) Div Recce Regt
Empfangsort: ~~BOURNE END, BUCKS~~
Army Post
Straße: ~~CORTEGAR~~
Land: ENGLAND
Landesteil (Provinz usw.

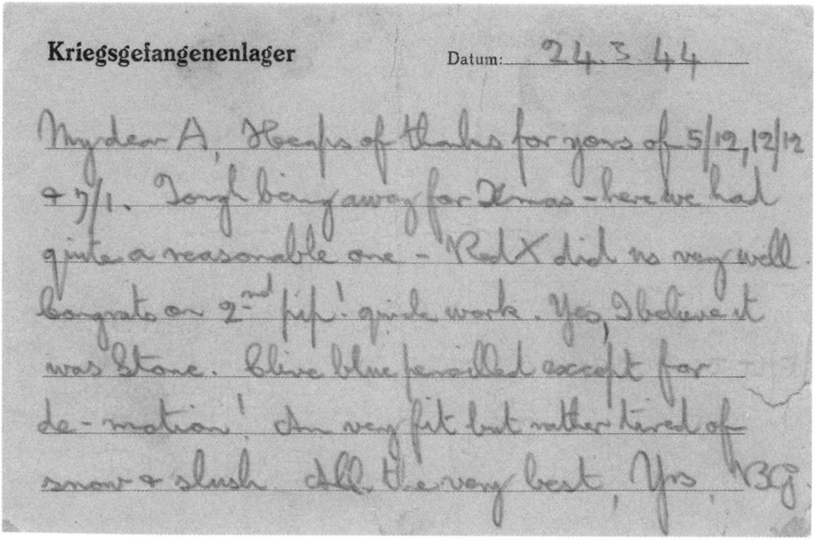
Kriegsgefangenenlager Datum: 24.3.44

My dear A, Heaps of thanks for yours of 5/12, 12/12 & 7/1. Tough being away for Xmas – here we had quite a reasonable one – Red X did us very well. Congrats on 2nd pip! good work. Yes, I believe it was Stone. Clive blue pencilled except for de-motion! Am very fit but rather tired of snow & slush. All the very best, Yrs, BG

with a chap called Mackintosh – one of the leading lights of the theatre – he gave masterly interpretation of "Higgins" in Pygmalion – is tall with long untidy hair (off the stage!) – told him it was a pity you weren't here in my place! Our room has frieze of all the posters of plays since theatre opened. Yes, I'm pretty well sure it was Stone – strongly built – medium height – fair. Am thinking of you more than usual these days, wondering what you will be up to. Congrats to Jim. I understand there may be a good chance of Thelma meeting her husband. Hear very good accounts of your health – keep it up! Am also very fit. I have certainly been more fortunate than the commandant of our special police though it has come to much the same in the end – do you remember his talk in the cinema at Marlow? I wonder where you will be when you get this letter. Every blessing. BG.

22.6.44 [Letter]

My dear Adrian, Very many thanks for yours of 14/2 & 14/3 – I suppose the tin trunk had to have a new lock fitted – am glad it is being made use of. Am wondering where you are now. Am very fit & trust you continue so. We had the film "orchestra Wives" yesterday – quite amusing in a light sort of way. Before that the theatre produced "I Killed the Count" – the standard here is amazingly high & that was well up to it. "Blithe Spirit" next week. I hear the Red X have sent us about 50 films so there will be no lack of entertainment. The posters of old plays are all round our room (I live with Mackintosh a leading light in the theatre) – no need to remember – going backwards they read – "Philadelphia Story", "Pygmalion", "arsenic & Old Lace", "Escape", "Tony draws a Horse", "Macbeth", "Rookery Nook", "design for Living", "George & Margaret" besides 4 Music Halls & 21 one-act plays by the Theatre Club! – I don't see much of Mackintosh as you can well imagine! The Theatre Club is a training ground for fresh actors – luckily I'm one of the few not connected with the theatre who get tickets – to my mind as good as other plays. All very best. BG.

29.8.44 [Postcard]

My dear A, Very many thanks for yours of 7/4 & 22/4. Am wondering what you've been up to since then! John Casson is producing "Saint Joan" shortly – he will probably make an excellent job of it – in the meantime we are expecting the film "Corsica Brother". Interested to hear of warehouse staff – thought it had been "demobbed"! All the very best. BG.

28.9.44 [Postcard]

My dear Adrian, Very many thanks for yours of 23/6. I hope you made a quick recovery. Am very fit. Here things go on as much as usual – John Casson's production of St Joan was immense success – it seems to me the height of dramatic art to impersonate a woman dressed as a man! Next big feature will be "Flashing Stream" do you know it? All the very best. BG.

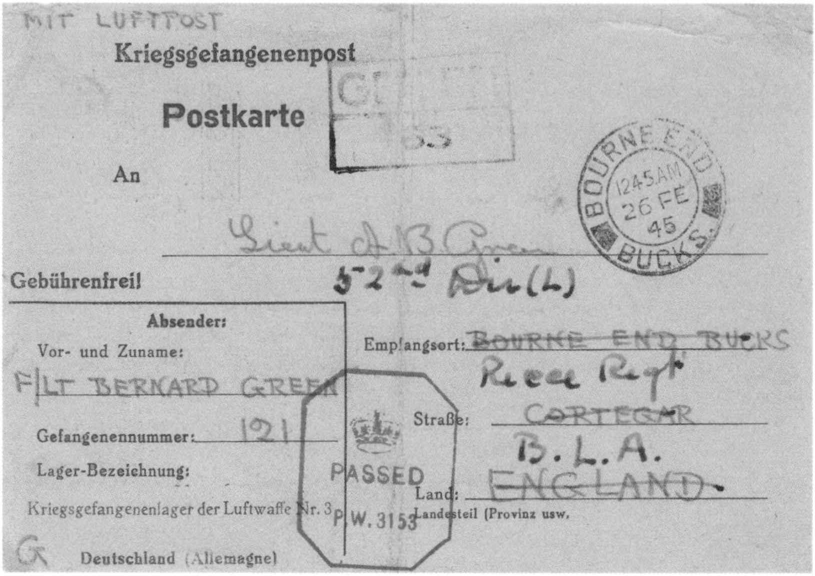

MIT LUFTPOST

Kriegsgefangenenpost

Postkarte

An

Lieut A B Green

52nd Div (L)

Gebührenfrei!

Absender:

Vor- und Zuname: F/LT BERNARD GREEN

Gefangenennummer: 121

Lager-Bezeichnung:

Kriegsgefangenenlager der Luftwaffe Nr. 3

Deutschland (Allemagne)

Empfangsort: ~~BOURNE END BUCKS~~ Recce Regt

Straße: ~~CORTEGAR~~

B.L.A.

Land: ~~ENGLAND.~~

Landesteil (Provinz usw.

PASSED P.W. 3153

BOURNE END BUCKS 12.45 AM 26 FE 45

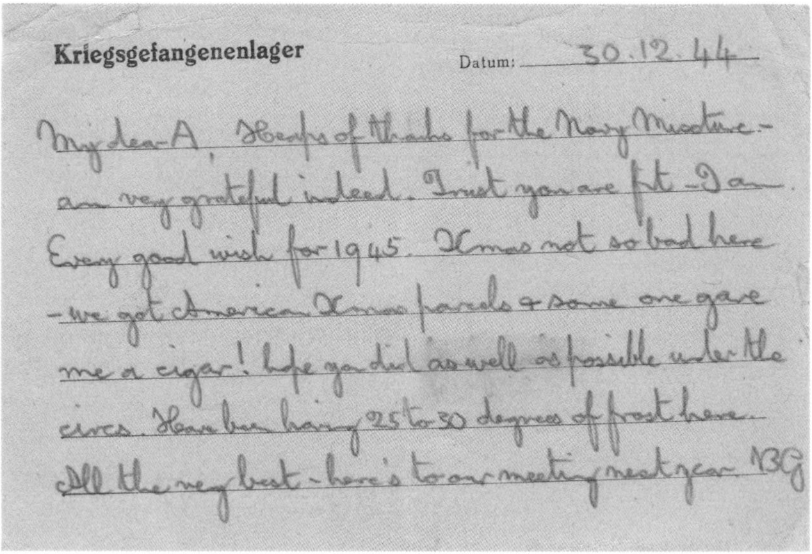

Kriegsgefangenenlager

Datum: 30.12.44

My dear A, Heaps of thanks for the Navy Mixture – am very grateful indeed. Trust you are fit – I am. Every good wish for 1945. Xmas not so bad here – we got American Xmas parcels & some one gave me a cigar! Hope you did as well as possible under the circs. Have been having 25 to 30 degrees of frost here. All the very best – here's to our meeting next year. BG

27.10.44 [Letter]

My dear Adrian, Very many thanks for yours of 1/8. Many happy returns of the day! One of my room mates – mackintosh, director of the theatre – is 10 days older than you. There are now 4 of us in the room another one being Greenhous who does a good bit of producing – he is producing "The Flashing Stream" during the week after next. Do you know it? I've read it & liked it – Mack says it's the best play of the last 100 years! "No Time for Comedy" was a flop – the only one – they took it off after the first night – I went to the dress rehearsal (I often do, as you can imagine) & I felt as though you were being given a series of lectures – there's a lot in the play though – apparently they gave it the wrong treatment! Trust you are fit, as I am. I rather understand that you will be seeing a good bit of things by the time you get this! Getting a bit cold already tho' we don't get severe winters in these parts – -12°C was the lowest last year. I'm hoping to help you celebrate next birthday. All the very best. BG.

30.12.44 [Postcard]

My dear A, Heaps of thanks for the Navy Mixture – am very grateful indeed. trust you are fit – I am. Every good wish for 1945. Xmas not so bad here – we got American Xmas parcels & some one gave me a cigar! Hope you did as well as possible under the circs. Have been having 25 to 30 degrees of frost here. All the very best – here's to our meeting next year. BG.

Appendix 7

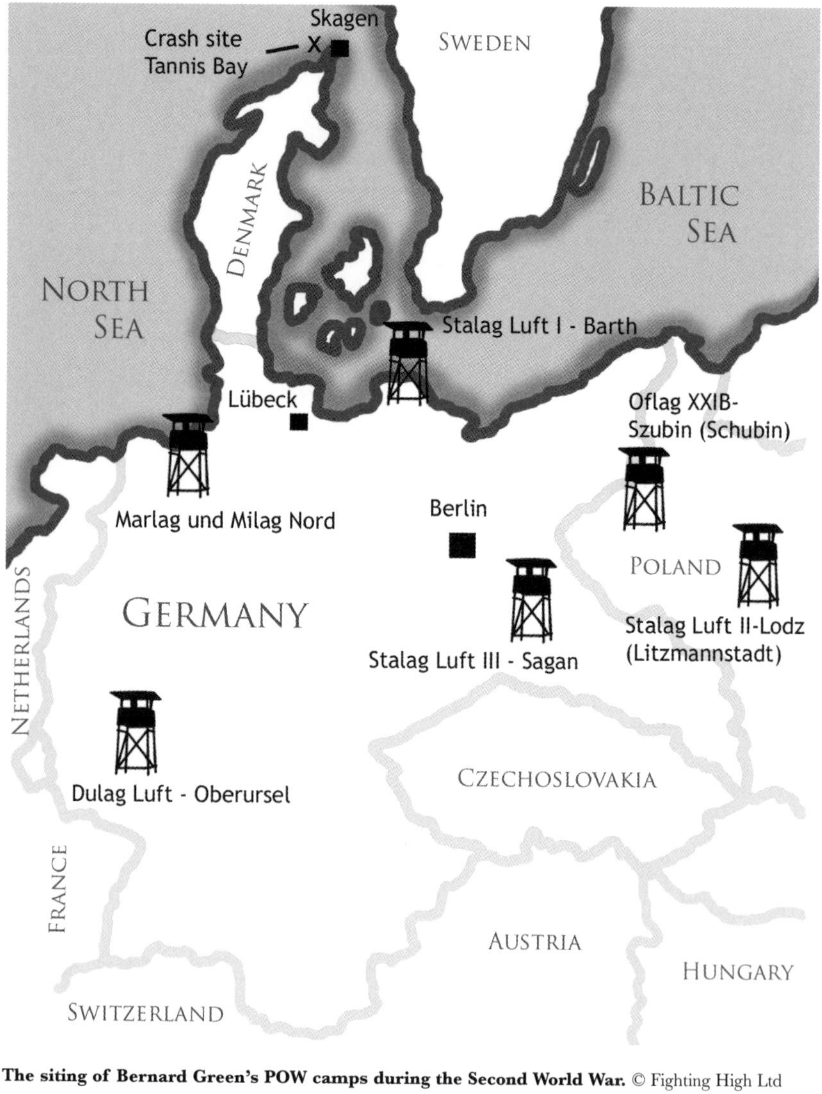

The siting of Bernard Green's POW camps during the Second World War. © Fighting High Ltd

Notes

Chapter 1: The Wild Rover No More

1. Silesia, the sandy somewhat barren area 100 miles south-east of Berlin, was known as Germany's desert. Goods manufactured in Silesia were known often to be of poor quality, hence the slang word 'sleasy'.
2. Sagan, a pretty, small town in German Silesia, became Zagan in 1945, when the whole of Silesia reverted to Poland and all Germans were deported. Since 1945 it has been in the province of Lubuskie in south-west Poland. It had 26,580 inhabitants in 2006.
3. The cooler was a block of single cells, each of which measured roughly 10 x 4 feet and was furnished with a bed, a chair and a bucket. Prisoners were sent for periods of two or three weeks' solitary confinement and fed through a flap in the door.
4. Major John 'Johnnie' Bigelow Dodge, DSO, DSC, MC (1894–1960), was known as 'the Artful Dodger'. A distant cousin by marriage to Winston Churchill, he was born an American citizen in New York City. He was commissioned into the Royal Naval Division in 1914 and became a British Citizen in 1915. He was wounded at Gallipoli, awarded the Distinguished Service Cross, and transferred to the British Army in 1916, where he rose to the rank of Acting Lieutenant Colonel, commanding the 16th Battalion of the Royal Sussex Regiment in France. He was wounded several times in the First World War and awarded the Distinguished Service Order. He travelled in China, Burma and Russia between the wars and spent two months in prison in the Caucasus in 1921 awaiting execution as a suspected spy. In 1939 he resumed the rank of Major in the

Middlesex Regiment. He was captured by the Germans at Saint-Valery-en-Caux, having attempted to swim out to some ships that were sailing away. He tried repeatedly to escape from various POW camps and was at every camp with Bernard Green except for Stalag Luft II. After the Great Escape he was sent to Sachsenhausen Concentration Camp, from where he escaped with 'Jimmy' James, 'Wings' Day and Sydney Dowse from Stalag Luft III and Jack Churchill. In February 1945 he was released from his chains in the Death Cell in the camp and sent by two senior German officials to Switzerland to negotiate a German surrender to the British and Americans using his assumed influence with Winston Churchill. The meeting took place two days after VE Day on 10 May 1945.

5. The 3rd Geneva Convention of 1929 covers prisoners of war. It states that prisoners must be adequately fed and have access to medical facilities. They were to wear appropriate articles of uniform and be allowed a set number of letters and postcards each month; both incoming and outgoing mail was to be censored. No POW was to be in the line of fire or aerial bombardment and was to be evacuated to a place of safety in a prompt manner. Officers and senior NCOs were not required to work unless they volunteered to do so. Other ranks were required to do so with the appropriate rates of pay. The Luftwaffe was the most independent service in Nazi Germany, the least influenced by Hitler's High Command. Their POW camps were generally run according to the Geneva Convention.

6. The Red Cross, headquartered in neutral Switzerland, relied on the adherence of warring nations to the Geneva Convention. Germany allowed it to visit POW camps but restricted access to concentration camps. The Red Cross traced military prisoners, arranged for parcels of food and clothes to be sent to all POW camps and enabled prisoners to keep in touch with their families at home. It had a much more limited success with concentration camps, where the Geneva Convention was generally flouted. British POWs relied on Red Cross food parcels to keep them alive. German rations, which were generally the same as were issued to camp guards, provided just over half the calories needed to keep an active man fit and well. Red Cross parcels made up the rest.

7. A 'goon' was RAF slang for a German guard or camp staff. It was based on the Popeye cartoon character 'Alice the Goon' and could be used as a noun, as in 'goon on the block', or an adjective, as in 'goon bread' (black bread). The word was explained to English-speaking guards and camp staff as 'German Officer Or Non-com'.
8. The Vorlager or 'front camp' was the administrative part of any POW camp. It generally contained the guardhouse and offices as well as the infirmary and the punishment block. All prisoners normally had to pass through the Vorlager before entering their compound, a fact that is ignored in the 1963 film *The Great Escape*.
9. The Machine Gun Corps was founded in October 1915 and consisted of three sections: Infantry, Cavalry and Motor branches. The Heavy section was formed in March 1916 to crew the first tanks, which were first in action at Flers during the Battle of the Somme in September 1916. The Infantry branch was the largest; battalion machine-gun sections were grouped into Brigade Machine Gun Companies, three in each division. In 1917 a fourth company was added, and in February 1918 the four companies in each division were formed into a Machine Gun Battalion. The gun teams used Vickers guns, which were developed from the Maxim guns still used by the German army. The lighter Lewis guns continued to be used at regimental level. Private Harry Patch of the Duke of Cornwall's Light Infantry was part of a Lewis gun team that was blown up by a German shell at Pilckem Ridge in 1917. Lieutenant Bernard Green of the Ox. and Bucks Light Infantry transferred to the MGC in early 1916. He kept his Sam Browne belt worn with two vertical straps according to Light Infantry practice, but wore the Machine Gun cap badge, which consisted of two crossed Vickers guns surmounted by a crown. He took two machine-gun courses at Belton Park, Grantham, and Camiers in France. He met Major 'Johnny' Dodge at one or both courses. Out of 170,500 officers and men who served in the Machine Gun Corps during the First World War, 62,049 became casualties, of which 12,498 were killed. The MGC was universally known as the 'Suicide Club'.
10. Nil illegitimi carborundum (dog Latin): 'Don't let the bastards grind you down' (anon.).

11. Appel was the twice-daily parade to count the prisoners and check numbers.
12. The Eagle squadrons, No. 71, No. 121, and No. 133, consisted of American pilots raised by Charles Sweeny in the USA. Sweeny and his wealthy friends contributed over $100,000 to send American pilots to Britain for training.
13. Bernard Green was a Theology student at Trinity College, Cambridge, from 1907 until 1910. He graduated with a third-class honours degree in 1910 (tripos).
14. Squadron Leader Roger Joyce Bushell, RAF (1910–44), was born in South Africa and educated at Wellington College before reading law at Pembroke College, Cambridge. He was an outstanding downhill skier who had a drooping left eye as the result of a skiing accident in Canada. He was fluent in French and German and became an auxiliary RAF officer in 1932 while pursuing his career as a lawyer. In 1939 he was given command of No. 92 Squadron and promoted to Squadron Leader in 1940, a few months before being shot down near Calais in his Spitfire. He was one of the few officers who had been 'in the bag' longer than Bernard Green. Bushell attempted to escape several times and developed a hatred for the Germans after bad treatment at the hands of the Gestapo in Prague. Known as 'Big X', he masterminded several escapes, the best known of which was from Stalag Luft III on 24 March 1944.
15. Bernard Green fought in the First, Second, and Third Battles of Ypres in Belgium and the Battle of the Somme in France.

Chapter 2: 'Prepare for Crash-landing'

1. No. 44 Squadron RAF, later known as No. 44 (Rhodesia) Squadron, was formed in 1917 as a home defence squadron. It was reformed in 1937 as a bomber squadron and moved to RAF Waddington near Lincoln, where it operated Handley Page Hampdens. It was one of only two squadrons to operate continuously throughout the war. In 1941 it was the first squadron to convert entirely to Lancasters and suffered the third highest casualty rate of RAF Bomber Command:
   Handley Page Hampden: 2,043 sorties (43 lost)
   Avro Lancaster: 4,362 sorties (171 lost).
2. Oxfordshire and Buckinghamshire Light Infantry. Both Adrian

Green and Bernard Green served in the Ox. and Bucks: Adrian as a Private and Lance Corporal, Bernard as Second Lieutenant, Lieutenant, Captain and Major in 1/1 Buckinghamshire Battalion, the senior battalion of all light infantry regiments. In 1916 Lieutenant Bernard Green was seconded to the Machine Gun Corps but continued to fight with the Ox. and Bucks, exchanging his 1/1 Ox. and Bucks cap badge for the crossed Vickers guns and crown of the MGC.

3. OCTU: Officer Cadet Training Unit.
4. Thomas and Green, Soho Mill, Wooburn Green, Bucks, is now mainly demolished and has become a number of industrial units. The company roll of honour from the First World War can still be seen there.
5. Handley Page Hampden Mark 1 was a medium two-engined bomber used mainly during the first three years of the Second World War. It was known to its four-man crews as the 'flying suitcase'. It was armed with four or six .303 Vickers K machine guns, and could carry either 4,000 lb of bombs, a single 18-inch torpedo or 4,000 lb of sea mines.
6. Flight sergeants were non-commissioned officers who performed all the jobs of air crew without the burden of mess bills, which were paid by all commissioned officers. Flight sergeants did not have to buy their uniforms or mess kit during wartime.
7. The RAF expression 'prang', meaning a crash or accident in the air, was coined by Pilot Officer Ernest Wakeham, RAF, DFC, from Rattery in south Devon. On a Devon farm a 'prang' is a two-tined pitchfork used mainly for tossing bales. It is said that Wakeham coined the term in the Church House Inn during a game of darts, where the word 'prang' referred locally to a 'double top'.
8. Denmark and Norway were invaded very rapidly by the Germans in the spring of 1940.
9. John Hampden (1595–1643), a relative of Oliver Cromwell, led Parliament in its opposition to ship money and to a war against the Scots. He believed that King Charles I was to be opposed on the grounds that he was attacking religion and the fundamental laws of England. He was mortally wounded at the Battle of Chalgrove Field in 1643.

10. Frederikshavn is a port on the Baltic coast of northern Denmark and the place where much of the iron ore from Sweden entered the domain of the Third Reich.
11. Handley Page Hampden Mark I L4087 ditched in the sea a few hundred yards off the village of Kandestierdne in Tannis Bay at 00.55 hrs on 20 July 1940. Ref: latitude 57.665 N, longitude 10.378 E.
12. Fritz Andersen had his sandals returned by Adrian Green and was sent a new trench coat by Bernard Green quite soon after the end of the war.
13. Skagen is the northernmost town in Denmark and a pretty place known for its painted wooden houses, its cobbled streets and its artists.

Chapter 3: In the Bag

1. A Luger is a German semi-automatic pistol used in both world wars. Bernard Green had acquired one in the trenches but patriotically handed it in to the British government in 1939.
2. German sentry boxes were decorated with stripes in the old imperial colours.
3. A Feldwebel was the German equivalent of a sergeant major or senior warrant officer.
4. 551536 Sergeant R. T. Miller, RAF, and 580671 Sergeant P. D. Nixon, RAF, were buried at Skagen cemetery on 24 and 25 July 1940. Between their graves is one of the damaged propellers from Handley Page Hampden L4087.
5. Dickens (rank unknown) was another of the coincidences that so delighted Bernard Green. He came from Marlow, Bucks, and lived in the next house to the Buckmaster family. Green's daughter married Lieutenant Clive Buckmaster of the Hampshire Regiment in 1942.
6. Group Captain Harry Melville Arbuthnot Day, RAF, GC, DSO, OBE (1898–1977), was Senior British Officer in most of the POW camps that Bernard Green was held in. He made escape attempts from Dulag Luft, Stalag Luft I, Stalag Luft III East Compound, Offlag XXIB, Stalag Luft III North Compound, Sachsenhausen Concentration Camp and Villa Bassa in the Tyrol. He was a clear case of an officer who should have been sent to Colditz. He was

known as 'Wings' Day, not because of his rank at the time but after an annual RAF charity event.

7. Dulag Luft (Durchgangslager der Luftwaffe) was the main transit camp for Air Force prisoners of war. It was situated at Oberusel, near Frankfurt, and acted as an interrogation centre for aircrews, who were then given a POW number and sent to different camps for officers and other ranks. It consisted of an old government poultry farm, which grew in size as a greater number of prisoners arrived. The main building, or 'stone house', was used as an interrogation centre when huts were built in the grounds.
8. Abort was the German word for toilet and considered rather indelicate by well-bred British officers.
9. Major Theo Rumpel was commandant of Dulag Luft from 1939 to 1941. He was respected as a fair man who tried to follow the Geneva Convention where humanly possible. He is reputed to have rewarded 'Wings' Day with a bottle of champagne for his first unsuccessful escape attempt.
10. SA chevrons on the left sleeve indicated that a soldier had been a member of the Sturmabteilung or 'brownshirts', the quasi-military organisation that helped bring Hitler to power in the 1920s and 1930s.
11. The North Compound of Stalag Luft III was outside Sagan in Upper Silesia. When the South Compound for American Air Force officers was completed, the whole camp was surrounded by over 5 miles of barbed-wire fencing.
12. 'Dhobying' was an old British Army term for washing clothes brought back by them from India.
13. Stalag Luft I was situated at Barth, in Mecklenburg–Western Pomerania near the Baltic Sea. It is said to have shielded the town of Barth from Allied bombing.

Chapter 4: In the Trenches

1. He was sent home for a month and then returned to active service.
2. The parados was the back wall of the trench.
3. 1 July 1916 was the first day of the Battle of the Somme. The British Army sustained 54,470 casualties on that day.
4. Chair bodgers made chairs out of green wood in the Chilterns in

Buckinghamshire.

5. Officers' brown polished leather sword belts were known as 'Sam Brownes'. The Light Infantry regiments wore theirs with two straps, one over each shoulder instead of one diagonal strap across the chest.

Chapter 5: Escape Plans

1. SS Obergruppenführer Reinhard Tristan Eugen Heydrich (1904–42). As Deputy Reich Protector of Bohemia and Moravia, he chaired the Wannsee Conference in 1942 that proposed the 'final solution' for Jews in German-occupied territories. He was attacked on 27 May 1942 by British-trained Czech agents and wounded by a hand grenade. He died over a week later. The German revenge on Czechoslovakia was brutal even by Nazi standards.
2. Flight Lieutenant Eric Williams, RAF, MC, and Lieutenant Michael Codner RA, MC.
3. Klim was powdered milk in tins from the USA and Canada, which came in Red Cross parcels. 'Klim' spelled 'milk' backwards.
4. The Baedeker raids were named after the famous German Baedeker guide books and concentrated on English towns and cities such as Exeter that were known for their beauty or historical associations.
5. 'Ferrets' were dedicated to finding escape tunnels and foiling escape attempts. They wore blue boiler suits and carried long steel rods for probing cavities. They also listened from rooftops and from under huts. The best-known ferret was Gefreiter (Senior Private) Greise, a.k.a. 'Rubberneck'.
6. A Gefreiter was the German equivalent of a senior private.
7. Offlag XXIB was situated at Schubin in Poland.
8. The North Compound of Stalag Luft III at Sagan was built by Russian slave labour. Early pictures of the compound show the tree stumps before they were all grubbed out for fuel.
9. Oberst (Colonel) Friedrich-Wilhelm von Lindeiner-Wildau (1881–1963) was commandant of Stalag Luft III from 1942 until 1944, replacing Oberst Stephani at the age of 61. He joined Goering's staff in 1937 and was not allowed to retire.
10. Kripo was the Nazi criminal police, which worked closely with the Gestapo.

11. Hauptmann (Captain) Broili was in charge of German security at the camp.
12. Hauptmann (Captain) Hans Pieber was Austrian and was respected for his correct treatment of POWs.
13. The tunnels were called Tom, Dick and Harry. Tom was discovered by the Germans in the summer of 1943, Dick was used for storage and sand dispersal and Harry was the tunnel through which the seventy-six Allied officers escaped on 24 and 25 March 1944.
14. The 'Mill Row' is dealt with fully in G. T. Mandl, *Three Hundred Years in Paper* (London, 1985), pp.188–93, 236–7.
15. *Triumph des Willens* (*'Triumph of the Will'*) was a German propaganda film made by Leni Riefenstahl. It won international acclaim and many awards for its revolutionary treatment of the 1934 Nuremberg Rally, which was attended by 30,000 people. It was partially directed by Adolf Hitler and shows him as the leader of a strong Germany that is regaining its dominant place in Europe.
16. See Page 131.
17. The South Compound of Stalag Luft III was opened in 1943 exclusively for American Air Force officers.
18. Flight Lieutenant George Harsh (1910–80), RCAF, was in charge of security until moved to the South Compound with other American officers. Before the war he had served a long prison sentence for murder.
19. A Bronx cheer was a euphemism for a fart.
20. c.230 tons of sand were excavated and hidden during the escape.
21. c.4,000 bed boards were used to shore up the sides of the tunnels. Many prisoners were forced to sleep on a frame of chicken wire beneath their palliasses.
22. Flight Lieutenant Paul Chester Jerome Brickhill (1916–91) was the Australian RAF officer who wrote *The Great Escape*.

Chapter 6: The Great Escape

1. See illustration in picture section.
2. Flying Officer Pawel Whilem Tobolski, Polish Squadron, RAF (1906–44), was dressed as a Wehrmacht corporal who was to accompany 'Wings' Day as his guard.
3. The bellows were invented by Squadron Leader Bob Nelson, RAF

(1915–99).

4. Green had been awarded his first Mention in Despatches in January 1917 for the part he played in the Battle of the Somme. The award is shown as a bronze oak leaf sewn onto the ribbon of the relevant campaign medal. He was awarded his second MiD in 1945 for his part in the escape.
5. The twelve men were: Bull, Dodge, Green, James, Kierath, Kiewnarski, Mondschein, Pawluk, Poynter, Skanziklas, Wernham, and Williams (John E.A.). Only Dodge, Green, James, and Poynter were not shot by the Gestapo.
6. Boberöhrsdorf was a small village on the same river (the Bober) as Sagan, but situated about 50 miles further south.
7. The Riesengebirge (Giant Mountains) lay between Green and Czechoslovakia to the south.
8. The Second Battle of Ypres.
9. Lieutenant Douglas Arthur Poynter, RN (Fleet Air Arm).
10. Green's MC was published in the *London Gazette* on 2 June 1918, King George V's official birthday. Because it was awarded in the birthday honours, there was no citation.
11. Flight Lieutenant Kenneth Mackintosh, RAF (1919–2006), was responsible for building the camp theatre at Sagan. After the war, he worked as a director at the National Theatre under Sir Laurence Olivier.
12. Group Captain Herbert Massey, RAF, CBE, DSO, MC (1898–1976), had replaced 'Wings' Day as Senior British Officer, because he outranked him. Massey had suffered a bad leg wound and was soon to be repatriated through Switzerland on medical grounds. In 1945 he was promoted to Air Commodore.
13. Birkland, Brettell, Bull, Bushell, Casey, Catanach, Christensen, Cochran, Cross, Espelid, Evans, Fuglesang, Gouws, Grisman, Gunn, Hake, Hall, Hayter, Humphreys, Kidder, Kierath, Kiewnarski, Kirby-Green, Kolanowski, Krol, Langford, Leigh, Long, McGarr, McGill, Marcinkus, Milford, Mondschein, Pawluk, Picard, Pohe, Scheidhauer, Skanziklas, Stevens, Stewart, Stower, Street, Swain, Tobolski, Valenta, Walenn, Wernham, Wiley, J. E. Williams, J. F. Williams.
14. Sachsenhausen Concentration Camp was situated in Oranienburg

in Germany, 35 miles north of Berlin. Day, Dodge, James and Dowse were placed in the Sonder-Lager, or special section for important prisoners, from which they escaped through a tunnel dug under the stone perimeter walls. They were all recaptured.

15. The Reconnaissance Corps was an elite corps founded in 1941 and disbanded in 1946. It was transferred from the infantry to the Royal Armoured Corps. The cap badge was an upright spear with two lightning flashes on each side. It was called Tannenbaum (Christmas tree) by German children.
16. V1s and later V2s.
17. Major Gustav Simoleit was Deputy Commandant of Stalag Luft III for the thirty-three months of its existence. He had been a professor of history, geography and ethnology before the war, spoke several languages fluently, and insisted on providing full military honours at the funerals of POWs, including a Jewish airman, against Hitler's orders.
18. Sous-Lieutenant Bernard Scheidhauer, Free French Air Force (1921–44).
19. Lieutenant Commander John Casson, RN (Fleet Air Arm), was shot down with Lieutenant Peter Fanshawe, RN (Fleet Air Arm), whom he helped at Sagan as one of the Escape Committee.

Chapter 7: The Black March

1. Feldwebel (Sergeant Major) Hermann Glemnitz was the senior NCO in charge of security. He had been a pilot in the First World War and was respected and feared by all. The only tunnel that escaped his discovery was Harry. He was a popular speaker at post-war POW reunions, where he was no longer referred to as 'that bastard Glemnitz'.
2. Group Captain Larry Wray RCAF (1908–77) had replaced Group Captain Massey as Senior British Officer before the 'Black March'. In 1955 he was promoted to Air Vice Marshal.
3. Marlag und Milag Nord was an abandoned camp for Royal Navy personnel at Westertimke, 23 miles north of Bremen, which had previously been condemned as unfit and unsanitary by the Red Cross.
4. On 2 May 1945 the camp was liberated by the Welsh Guards, who

were part of 11th Armoured Division, Second Army.

5. The two white kitbags were used for years to collect stale bread for geese. I still have one of them.

Bibliography

World War Two Prisoner of War Camps*

Brickhill, Paul. *The Great Escape*. London: Faber, 1963.

Carroll, Tim. *The Great Escapers*. Edinburgh: Mainstream, 2004.

Clutton-Brock, Oliver. *Footprints on the Sands of Time*. London: Grub Street, 2002.

Gilbert, Adrian. *POW: Allied Prisoners in Europe*. London: John Murray, 2006.

James, B. A . 'Jimmy', in *Moonless Night*. Barnsley: Leo Cooper, 2002.

Rees, Ken, with Arrandale, Karen. *Lie in the Dark and Listen*. London: Grub Street, 2004.

Rollings, Charles. *Prisoner of War*. London: Ebury Press, 2007.

Williams, Eric. *The Wooden Horse*. London: Fontana, 1953.

Williams, Eric. *The Tunnel*. Barnsley: Pen and Sword, 2007.

Wilson, Patrick. *The War behind the Wire*. Barnsley: Pen and Sword, 2000.

** There are inaccuracies about Flight Lieutenant Bernard Green in almost all the books where he is mentioned.*

First World War

Ellis, John. *Eye-Deep in Hell: Life in the Trenches 1914–1918*. London: Fontana, 1977.

Gibbs, Philip. *Now It Can Be Told*. London: Harper, 1920.**

Hart, Peter. *The Somme*. London: Weidenfeld and Nicolson, 2005.

Holmes, Richard. *The Western Front*. London: BBC, 1999.

Macdonald, Lyn. *Somme*. London: Macmillan, 1985.

O'Shea, Stephen. *Back to the Front*. London: Robson Books, 1996.

*** Bernard Green had probably read this book and borrowed the title for the short account of his recapture.*

Papermaking

Mandl, George T., *Three Hundred Years in Paper*. London: P and M, 1985.

Index